RnB**SOUL**&**MOTOWN** STYLE**BASSLINES**

Learn 100 Bass Guitar Grooves in the Style of the Soul Legends

DAN**HAWKINS**

FUNDAMENTAL**CHANGES**

RnB, Soul & Motown Style Basslines

Learn 100 Bass Guitar Grooves in the Style of the Soul Legends

ISBN: 978-1-78933-243-8

Published by **www.fundamental-changes.com**

www.fundamental-changes.com

Over 11,000 fans on Facebook: **FundamentalChangesInGuitar**

Instagram: **FundamentalChanges**

For over 350 Free Guitar Lessons with Videos Check Out

www.fundamental-changes.com

Contents

Introduction

The Rhythm and Blues (RnB), Soul, and Motown music that emerged from the US in the late '50s and early '60s made legends of a number of bass players whose influence still remains strong today. This book focuses on the lines and grooves of the great players of the early '60s onwards, who were mainly from Detroit, Memphis, Muscle Shoals, Philadelphia, New York and Chicago, where these styles took hold. They churned out hit after hit, often not receiving any credit for their work. In fact, don't be surprised if you haven't heard of all the players in this book (although you'll have definitely heard their playing).

When you consider that Leo Fender's first Precision basses passed into the hands of the jazz double bass players of the late '50s, then listen to the basslines of the early RnB pioneers, you'll quickly hear that it was a special era for music indeed. And now, when you listen to the new era of bass superstars like Joe Dart, you'll realise how heavily these early pioneers have influenced future generations.

Soul music teaches you so much about groove, musicality and song construction, so along with learning one hundred cool bassline ideas, this book teaches you the inner workings of the style and will help you create your own authentic basslines and fills.

When working through this book it's important to immerse yourself in the styles covered, so to help you out I've created a Spotify playlist for you that covers all the important players, feels and grooves. Make this the soundtrack to your day and the groove will get into you by pure osmosis!

Each example in this book has a corresponding audio example that you can download for free from **www.fundamental-changes.com** and many also have backing tracks for you to play along to. These will help you develop your timing and give you the opportunity to practice the ideas more musically

Ultimately, this collection of grooves, breakdowns and fills will put you on the fast train to Detroit and you'll master the Motown groove in no time!

Have fun!

Dan

Get the Spotify playlist to accompany this book now by scanning the QR code:

Get the Audio

The audio files for this book are available to download for free from **www.fundamental-changes.com.** The link is in the top right-hand corner. Simply select this book title from the drop-down menu and follow the instructions to get the audio.

We recommend that you download the files directly to your computer, not to your tablet, and extract them there before adding them to your media library. You can then put them on your tablet, iPod or burn them to CD. On the download page there is a help PDF and we also provide technical support via the contact form.

For over 350 free lessons with videos check out:

www.fundamental-changes.com

Join our active Facebook community:

www.facebook.com/groups/fundamentalguitar

Tag us for a share on Instagram: **FundamentalChanges**

Getting the Sound

Almost all the players in this book used a Fender Precision bass. It's one of life's great mysteries how Leo Fender got the design and sound of this instrument so right the first time around. There were a few alterations and updates made from the initial 1951 release but by the early 1960s most bassists gravitated towards playing the models of the late '50s and early '60s.

The other mainstay of the sound was using flatwound strings, which have a smooth winding around the core and are similar to the double bass strings early pioneers would have been used to. LaBella flatwounds were popular and you can still buy them today. Along with the foam mutes commonly found on early Precision basses, those strings contributed to a slightly muted yet round tone that sat perfectly in the mix.

In 1957 the split coil pickup was added. The thick, warm tone this gave was the sound producers and listeners alike became accustomed to. It's also a tone that has come back into fashion since the '80s.

You don't need to spend $10,000 on a vintage bass to get the tone, as most basses are now modelled on a Fender Precision or Jazz bass. In fact, after-market gear such as Fender's own Custom Shop 1962 Precision pickup make it even easier to accurately emulate the classic Motown tone.

To emulate the sound of the foam that was originally placed on the underside of the chrome bridge cover, you can place some foam under the strings right by the bridge or tape some felt over the top of the strings.

The most commonly used amp was the Ampeg B15, but in fact many engineers plugged the bass straight into the mixing desk and used the desk's onboard preamps to boost the signal. That's how the famous Motown sound was achieved. If you're practicing or playing live, any tube amp with a fifteen-inch speaker can deliver something close to the classic 1960s tone.

Don't get too hung up on the gear though. You can use any bass you have to hand and that will be absolutely fine to learn on.

Chapter One – Early Soul and RnB

Rhythm and Blues originally referred to the music being played by artists of the 1950s but by the 1960s, Soul music was dominating the RnB charts. The music combined elements of Gospel, Jazz, Blues and RnB, with bass and drums providing a rhythmic focal point, although around this time, the double bass was still the primary low-end instrument played on records. The transition from double to electric bass paved the way for all subsequent styles of modern music. These early players were influential beyond anything they could have conceived.

Perhaps the best proponent of RnB upright was Lloyd Trotman who played on many hits including Ben E. King's *Stand by Me*. He was a session player for one of the giant labels of Soul music, Atlantic Records, and his simple but memorable playing often provided the anchor for large ensembles.

Despite being there at the dawn of the bass guitar, Trotman played upright for Alan Freed's Rock and Roll Orchestra and recorded with Duke Ellington, Ray Charles, James Brown, Sam Cooke and countless others.

The music of this era had simple basslines, often outlining just the root of the chord while using notes from the key to link the chords musically. This resulted in memorably melodic, but simple phrases.

However, all that changed with the arrival of James Brown, the Godfather of Soul.

There aren't too many artists who can boast that they pioneered an entire style of music but in fact Brown can claim to have pioneered two! As his nickname suggests, he was pretty much the creator of Soul, but he also opened the door to Funk in the late '60s. Until Funk's first moment (*Cold Sweat* in 1967), Brown was dominating the RnB charts with hits such as *Night Train* and *Out of Sight*.

Brown always attracted great musicians and one of his best bass players was Bernard Odum. He played in Brown's band for around a decade from 1958, playing a prominent role in songs such as *Papa's Got A Brand New Bag* as well as *Cold Sweat*.

Gear Checklist

Lloyd Trotman played a German-made double bass throughout his career. Bernard Odum played a 1956 Fender Precision strung with flatwound strings.

Recommended Listening

Play It Fair – LaVerne Baker

Stand by Me – Ben E. King

Reet Petite – Jackie Wilson

Papa's Got A Brand New Bag – James Brown

I Got You (I Feel Good) – James Brown

Wee Wee – James Brown

Lloyd Trotman

Our first example is based around *Stand by Me* with its simple major scale pattern. Many basslines from this era used root notes to outline chords plus passing note from the scale.

In Example 1a, root notes are used on each chord, along with a simple rhythm.

Example 1a

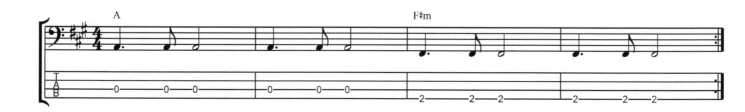

Taking the same chord progression (A to F#m) and adding a few notes from the scale, we can add melodic interest to the line. Keep your first finger hovering over the 2nd fret so that you can reach the notes on the 4th.

Example 1b

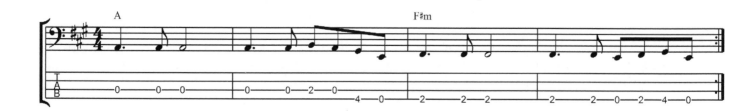

Songs of the time were often written in a 6/8 time signature where there are six 1/8th notes in every bar, grouped into two sets of three. To count this feel, tap your foot two-to-the-bar, feeling three 1/8th notes per tap. Example 1c stays in the key of A Major, and again uses notes from the scale to connect the roots. Make sure to play the tied notes for their full length.

Example 1c

The Blues features prominently in early RnB, with classic Willie Dixon style patterns played over the familiar I IV V chord progressions and Example 1d uses major triads played in a Blues style. A good example of this approach can be heard on *Play It Fair* by LaVern Baker.

Take the patterns below and rearrange the order of notes to create your own lines. Make sure you take your time to digest these shapes and try to memorise all of them. They show up in many styles of music!

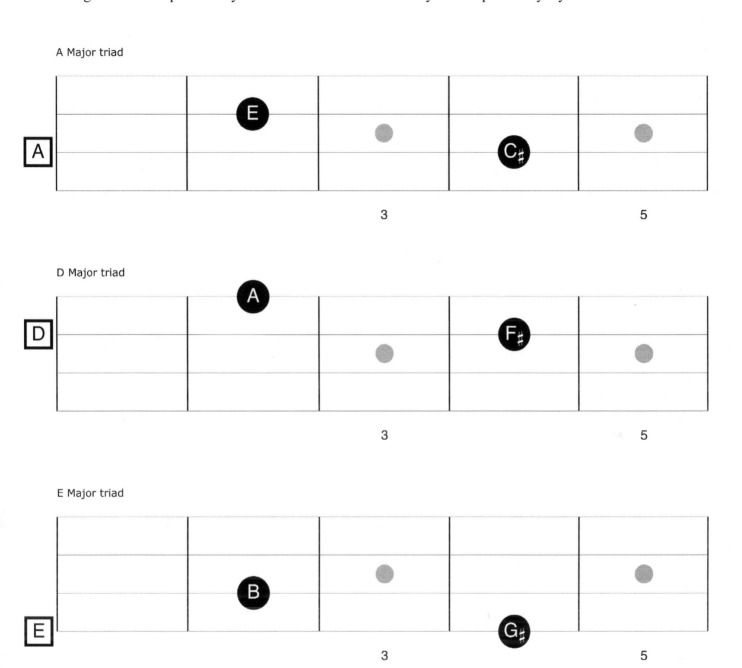

Example 1d

Soul bass is a style based squarely around patterns that usually highlight the notes of chords. If you learn the pattern *and* the sound, you'll get a long way towards being able to easily figure out basslines as well as how to create your own. Example 1e uses the Major 6th and an octave added onto the previous triad pattern to create yet another well-known line.

These are the shapes and you can hear Trotman playing them on *Reet Petite* by Jackie Wilson. All these notes come from scales, so make sure you know the major scale off by heart.

A Major 6th pattern

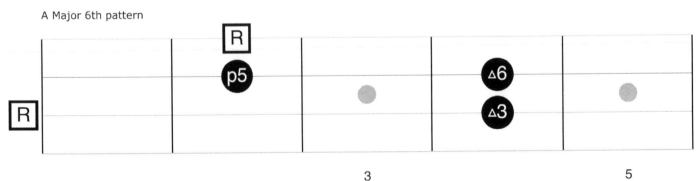

E Major 6th pattern

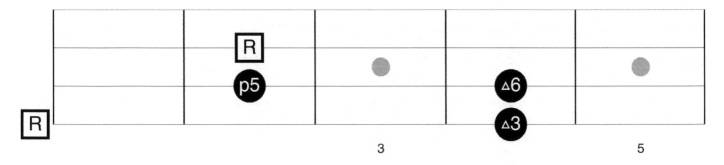

Example 1e

Bernard Odum

By the time Odum started playing with James Brown, basslines were becoming busier and more of a musical focal point in a song. Bassists started playing notes other than the roots and Example 1f highlights this by using the root, b7 and 5th.

Study the pattern below. Notice how the 5th is played below the root (the square) – something that happens a lot in bass playing. Memorise this shape, as you will come across it many times and it can be used over a dominant *or* a minor 7th chord as both chords contain these intervals.

Root, b7, 5th pattern

Example 1f

The next example takes the same line but now leads up to the root chromatically. *Chromatic* notes lie outside of the key or chord but add colour to lines. Using chromatic notes is a concept we will return to later in the book.

Example 1g

Two Odum basslines have confused bass players for years! Both *Papa's Got A Brand New Bag* and *I Got You (I Feel Good)* contain a Major 7th in the bassline despite the chord containing a Minor 7th. This shouldn't work but it does! It's just one example of an apparent clash of notes creating enough tension to make the music sound edgy and different.

Example 1h uses this idea over two dominant chords (which contain a b7).

Example 1h

Despite the Major 7th sorcery seen in the previous example, it's a good idea to familiarise yourself with a dominant arpeggio. Many Soul, RnB and Motown basslines use this harmony which comes, again, from the blues. Here's a D7 arpeggio.

D7 Arpeggio (D, F#, A, C, D)

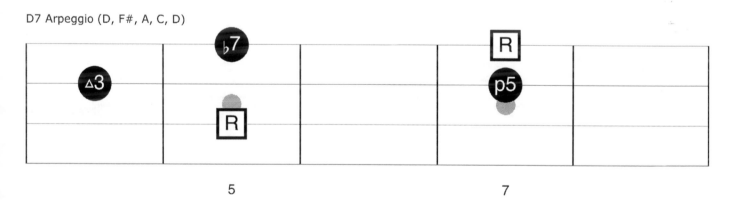

Example 1i takes this shape and outlines the D7 chord. Since this shape is movable, once you know the shape, move it around to outline different chords. Try singing the notes of the arpeggio away from your bass so you internalise the sound. This is fantastic ear training that enables you to quickly recognise different musical elements. Try this with scales, triads and arpeggios.

Example 1i

Now notice what happens when you combine these shapes with a consistent, repetitive rhythm – you create a groovy bassline! Look out for the 1/16th notes! Don't rush them and play them with alternate plucking. If the rhythms look tricky, give the audio example a listen.

Example 1j

Chapter Two – Memphis Soul and Stax

Memphis Soul is a popular sub-genre that gained in popularity during the 1960s and 1970s. It influenced many rock musicians of the time and was perhaps best characterised by the music made by Stax Records. They were one of *the* major Soul labels, second only in sales to Detroit's Motown.

Based out of Memphis, Stax created music based on early RnB, Gospel, Blues and Country. Their use of one studio and one group of musicians melded an unmistakable sound full of grease and character.

Despite early RnB and Soul largely describing the experience of black people in America, Stax featured house bands with racially integrated musicians. None made more of an impact than the label's in-house band Booker T. & the M.G.'s with their iconic bass player, Donald "Duck" Dunn.

However, Lewie Steinberg was the original bass player for the group. He recorded for them between 1962 and 1965, playing on one of the most famous instrumental tunes of all time, *Green Onions*.

It was Dunn who played on thousands of records for Stax and his influence as a bass player is monumental. He grew up in Memphis with the guitarist Steve Cropper and together they formed the nucleus of the Stax house band. Their playing is unmistakable and they had the ability to stamp their signature on any record. Without a doubt, these guys were integral in millions of record sales.

Dunn's playing was solid as a rock and he loved to create signature riffs that he would sit on for whole sections. He didn't play too many fills and instead relied on feel and tone to express his creativity.

Tommy Cogbill was another Tennessee native with a huge Soul legacy. He was closely associated with another southern Soul label, American Sound Studio and their house band, The Memphis Boys. He also recorded in Nashville, New York and Muscle Shoals.

He was a brilliant bass player with a busy, flowing style based more on improvisation and instinct. No bassline highlights this more than Dusty Springfield's *Son of a Preacher Man* (check out that outro!) He liked to infuse his lines with rhythmic 1/16th notes phrases while always supporting the vocals and locking in with the drums.

Such was the reach of his playing that the great Jaco Pastorius cited Cogbill as an influence. Jaco would often quote Cogbill's line on Wilson Pickett's *Funky Broadway*. Listen to that song and you can hear the influence of Memphis Soul on the Funk basslines that would soon emerge in the late 1960s. For more info and grooves, check out my book ***100 Funk Bass Grooves for Electric Bass***.

Gear Checklist

Duck used a 1959 Fender Precision strung with heavy gauge La Bella flatwounds and a one-piece maple neck. This was his second P bass after his first (which had a rosewood neck) was lost. Later in his career, Lakland released a Duck Dunn signature model based on his vintage Fender. He mostly played through Ampeg amplifiers.

1959 was a good year for Precisions. Amercian Sound Studios had one as the house bass for the studio and that was the one Tommy Cogbill used for most of his recordings.

Recommended Listening

Green Onions – Booker T. & the M.Gs

Jelly Bread – Booker T. & the M.Gs

These Arms of Mine – Otis Redding

Knock on Wood – Eddie Floyd

In the Midnight Hour – Wilson Pickett

B-A-B-Y – Carla Thomas

Son of a Preacher Man – Dusty Springfield

Memphis Soul Stew – King Curtis

Funky Broadway – Wilson Pickett

Lewie Steinberg

Green Onions was the most famous song Steinberg played on and it featured a distinctive Blues riff over a minor Blues progression. Example 2a uses a similar idea in the key of G Minor. Here we see another common pattern: the root, b3 and b7. This pattern is moved to the roots of each chord in the example.

Memorise the pattern and know which interval is which. You might recognise the *Rock Steady* (Aretha Franklin) bass riff within these funky notes.

Minor blues pattern (Gm)

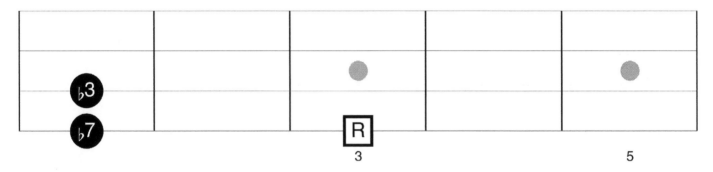

Example 2a has a swing 1/8th note feel, a classic Blues rhythm often heard in Soul. Listen to the audio example to hear it in action. Lock into the feel of the backing track to nail the swung 1/8ths.

Example 2a

17

You can use the same backing track for the next example.

Here, there's a slightly different pattern than before. This time it's root, 5th, b7 and octave and you'll find these intervals used *a lot* in bass playing. They crop up in everything from Blues to Funk and, of course, Soul. Keep the 1/8ths as steady as you can. You will come across this pattern many times as a bass player.

Root, 5th, b7, octave pattern (Gm)

Since you're using the same patterns throughout, keep your hand in the same shape and shift confidently to each new root.

Example 2b

The next example illustrates Steinberg's Lloyd Trotman-inspired use of simple notes in a major key. Play everything in first position and use your fourth finger for notes on the 3rd fret to lessen the stretch. You can use your third finger if you prefer.

The rhythms are syncopated so make sure to tap your foot on the beats as the tied notes land where your foot rises. If you get used to matching offbeats with your foot like that, they will become much easier to play. Use the backing track to help you practice your counting.

Example 2c

Example 2d is a slow 12/8 feel. This type of line looks easy enough but can be hard to play authentically as you need be in complete control of your inner clock. Count the beats throughout and play every note with authority. Playing in 12/8 means subdividing the bar into four groups of three 1/8th notes. Tap your foot as you normally would in 4/4 but feel three 1/8th notes per beat. This is a classic Soul ballad feel which you can master with the backing track.

Example 2d

The next example uses the same chord progression with yet another important Soul bass pattern of a moveable shape containing the root, 5th and Major 6th. You may recognise this sound from countless Blues and Soul songs. It's a great one to memorise and practice with the same backing track as the previous example.

Root, 5th, Major 6th pattern (Bb)

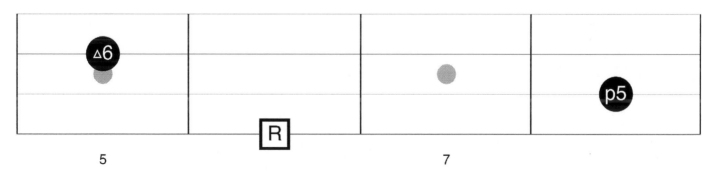

While you're playing along to the backing track, experiment by altering the rhythms as well as the order of the notes within the pattern. This is an easy way to come up with interesting new lines and keep things fresh.

Example 2e

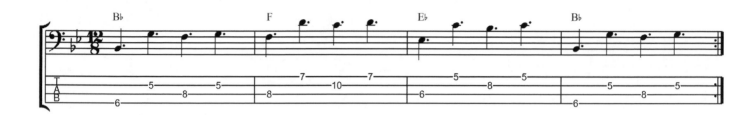

Donald "Duck" Dunn

When I think of Soul bass I think of Donald Dunn. Such is his importance to the genre that I've included *fifteen* grooves based around his style (I extend the same courtesy to James Jamerson later).

Dunn was a huge fan of simple repetitive patterns that locked in tightly with the drums. Example 2f uses this approach with a pattern he loved to play. Hundreds of famous basslines contain the notes within this pattern and you should recognise a few and try to use them in your own basslines.

Root, 5th, Major 6th pattern (Bb)

Play all the notes in Example 2f in first position. Use your fourth or third finger for the notes on the 3rd fret, whichever you find more comfortable.

Example 2f

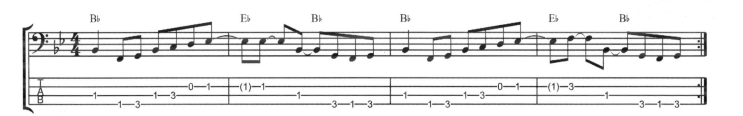

Knock on Wood contains one of the most famous basslines of all time. It's another root, 5th, Major 6th masterpiece and the next example uses the same notes. It's important to control the note length of the open strings and to do this, gently touch your fingers against the string to dampen them. At the same time, get your first finger ready to fret the next note.

Example 2g

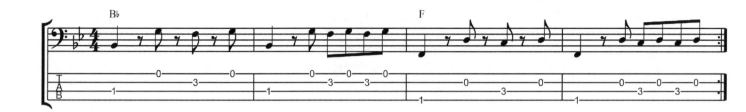

There's a hammer-on in the next example to watch out for. Use either your third or fourth finger for the hammer and aim to play everything in one position. However, if you prefer, you can quickly shift down to the 1st fret for the Bb.

Example 2h

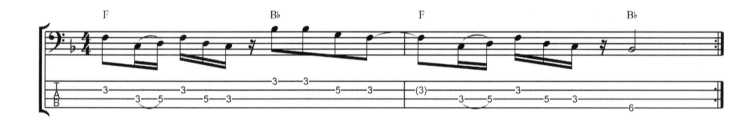

Dunn loved to use *articulations* like slides and hammer-ons. Soul basslines are often harmonically simple, so it's the tone and feel that needs to elevate the bassline. Feel often comes from solid timing and interesting articulations that add the soul and flair.

Here's another useful pattern, the Major Pentatonic scale. Notice that the major triad with the added Major 6th pattern from before can be found within this shape.

Play the pattern from the lowest note up. It's similar to the intro to *My Girl* and a good way to internalise the sound of this important scale.

Major Pentatonic scale (C)

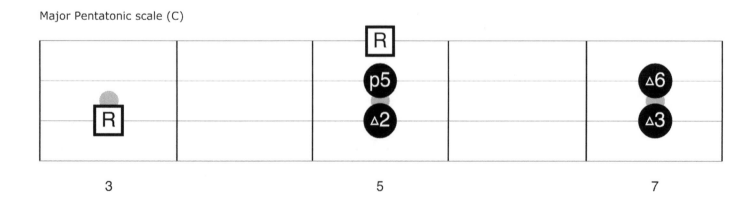

Playing notes on the same string allows you to add slides and hammer-ons, as demonstrated in this example. Start with your first finger on the 3rd fret then slide from 3 to 5 using your third finger. This brings you into position to play the remaining notes without having to shift.

Example 2i

Adding one note (the b3) to a Major Pentatonic scale creates the Major Blues scale. This simple addition adds a lot of juicy possibilities! Here's the diagram. Memorise the Major Pentatonic first as it will make this next groove much easier to learn.

Major Blues scale (C)

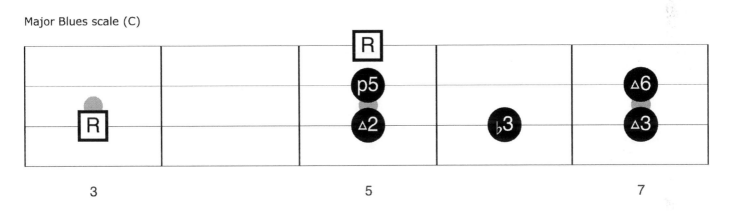

Let's take the previous line and add our new blues note. Play both examples one after the other to visualise where the b3 occurs but also to hear what effect it has on the sound. Loads of Soul and Blues basslines use this idea.

Example 2j

The influence of the Blues on Soul bass was monumental. Blues scales help to infuse other styles of music into Soul and it's a familiar and incredibly cool sound. The line in Example 2k bends the major second up a half step to the b3. To do this, push the 5th fret down towards the floor with your third and fourth fingers. You'll need a little strength to do this, so isolate those notes and practice them.

Listen to the audio example to catch the timing and feel.

Example 2k

Blues harmony is normally based around dominant chords which are built from the Mixolydian scale. Here's a diagram showing the Mixolydian scale, which highlights the dominant 7 arpeggio built from it with hollow circles. Lots of basslines can be derived from this scale so learn it well.

Mixolydian mode (Bb)

Example 2l uses the root, 5th, Major 6th bassline from previous examples along with the addition of a b7. Adding the b7 strongly outlines the dominant 7 harmony. Use the one-finger-per-fret technique so that your fingers line up starting on the 5th fret. Ensure you have a finger hovering over the next note before you play it to help with your timing and fluency.

Example 2l

Here's a line that uses notes from the Mixolydian over a 12-bar blues progression. The patterns are the same throughout so memorise them as you go, then shift your second finger to each new root note.

Example 2m

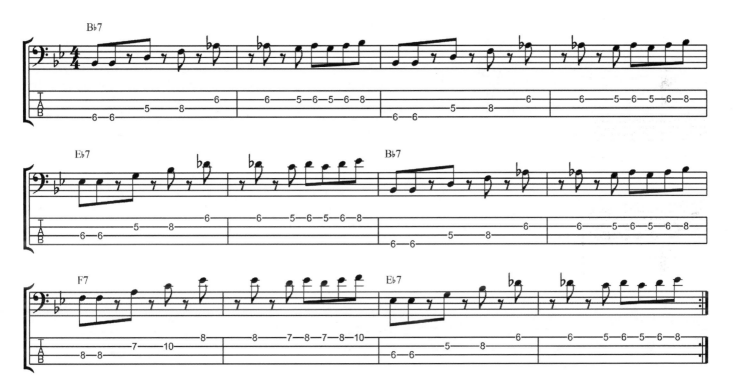

Even though dominant chords contain a Major 3rd, a Minor 3rd can be used as a passing note. This is something you hear a lot in Soul bass playing and it sounds awesome! Here's the pattern.

3

The next example shows you the tension this creates as the "wrong" b3 resolves to the "correct" Major 3rd. This is another extremely common Soul and RnB bass feature and you can use this idea in your lines.

Example 2n

This pattern sounds equally good up the octave. Here's the same line played around the 8th fret. Use the rest at the end of bar one to quickly shift your hand into place with your first finger at the 8th fret on the G string.

Example 2o

The next example uses simple roots and 5ths to create a melodic bassline. Listen to *(Sittin' On) the Dock of the Bay* for a great example of how effective this can be. The intro to *My Girl* played by James Jamerson is even more recognisable.

I find it much easier to play notes fretted on the 5th fret than open strings, as it's easier to control the note length and keep the tone consistent. You do need to be able to shift quickly though.

First, play the line as written in the notation, then transfer the open G and D strings to the 5th fret of the D and G strings respectively.

Example 2p

Lots of music from this period features bright-sounding dominant chords, but songwriters didn't forget minor chords! Here's a ii V progression in the key of Ab (Bbm7 to Eb7). Over the Eb7 chord at the end of bar two, another famous Soul pattern is in evidence. It's the walk up chromatically from the Major 3rd to the 5th and uses this shape:

Chromatic walk up from the Major 3rd to 5th (Eb)

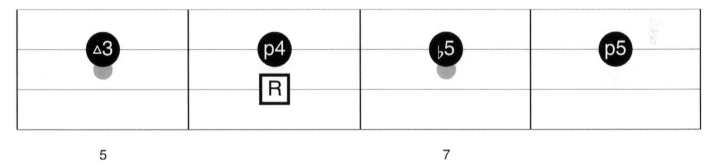

Play the Eb on the 6th fret with your second finger, so that you can then play the next notes one finger per fret. Then shift back quickly to be ready for the repeat. The tempo of this line is quite slow, so the 1/16th notes aren't as fast as they might look on paper. Check out the audio example to hear the groove.

Example 2q

Here's the same line again with the same pattern but this time down an octave. The following diagram shows the pattern with the shape going up and down from the root.

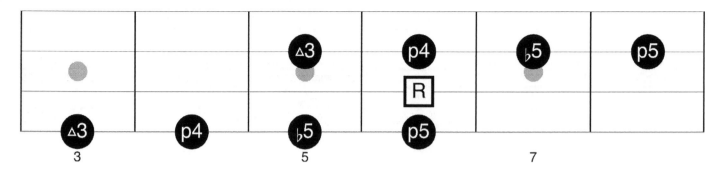

The pattern can be heard at the end of bar four and it leads satisfyingly back to the Bb root on the repeat. Memorise the patterns above and improvise your own lines by playing a rhythm on the root (Eb) then walking up from the Major 3rd to the 5th (using both positions).

Listen to Jaco Pastorius and you'll hear the huge influence Soul had on his playing!

Example 2r

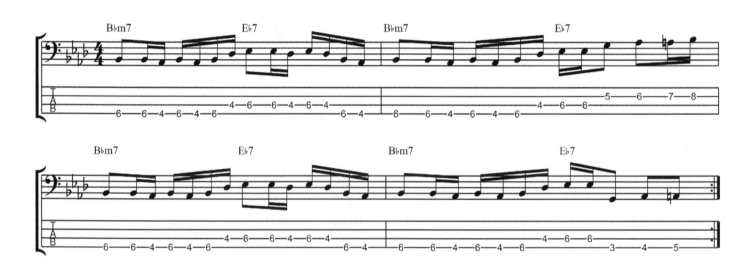

Dunn's basslines would often double up with horn riffs, a good example being the intro to *Knock on Wood*. The next example starts with a riff before adding some chromatic movement. There are a couple of hand shifts required to make the line sound smooth and connected, so follow the fingering suggestions closely, paying attention to the shift at the end of bar two.

Focus on your fourth finger as you make the move, then on your first finger as it targets the 5th on the lead up to the repeat. Start moving your first finger into position as your fourth finger plays the tied Bb on the 6th fret. Use your third finger instead of the fourth in bar one if you find it easier.

Example 2s

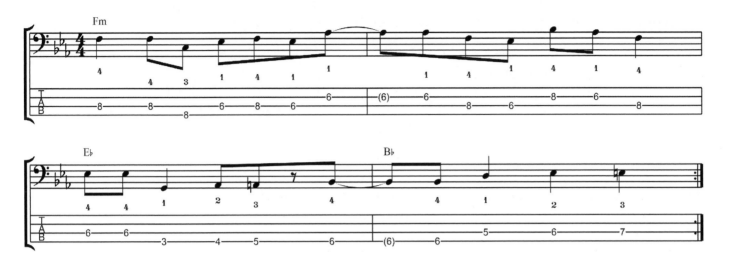

The next example sits on a C7 chord throughout and includes some fast plucking and a hammer-on. Watch out for the 1/16th notes, making sure to use alternate plucking before using your first and second fingers for the hammer-on in the following bar. Notice that chromatic movement making another appearance.

Example 2t

Tommy Cogbill

Cogbill played on one of the most famous Soul songs of all time, King Curtis' *Memphis Soul Stew*. The intro is just one note but it's played with incredible groove and feel.

The next example focuses on the root note of an E7 chord. Notice how much life the syncopated 1/16th note rhythms bring to one solitary note.

Tap your foot on each beat while counting 1/16th notes. You can count "one e and a two e and a three e and a four e and a..." It's essential you keep this counting going so it becomes completely natural and internalised. Building up that internal *grid* is a great way to cultivate your groove. Set a metronome to a slow tempo and work on these types of rhythms daily.

They're tricky to play, so listen to the audio examples a few times before diving in.

Example 2u

Example 2v adds a little melody to the previous line. Play the Es in bar three with your first finger so you're in position for the notes in bar four. Tommy Cogbill was an incredibly dextrous player and used a lot of alternate plucking. You can also use raking in the final bar to execute the phrase. As long as it's precise and bang in time, it doesn't matter what technique you use.

Example 2v

One of the greatest riffs of all time is *Funky Broadway* by Wilson Pickett. Cogbill's light touch and hip use of both minor and major harmony helped to create something truly special. The next example is in a similar style and there's a lot to pay attention to!

Hammer on to the 2nd fret with your first finger then lightly pull the G on the E string down towards the ground. Next, slide into the 4th fret on the A string with your third finger to get you in position to play the remaining notes one finger per fret.

The key to playing this riff authentically is nailing those articulations and playing with complete coordination between the hands. You might want to slow this one down and piece it together bit by bit. Don't try to get it up to speed until you have everything together.

Example 2w

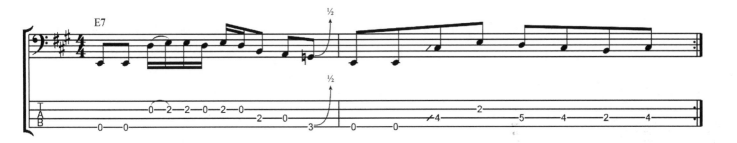

The next example has two patterns that you can use to create your own fills and basslines. You can use the backing track to practice your riff writing. Let's look at the shapes. Over the G chord, use this G Major Pentatonic pattern.

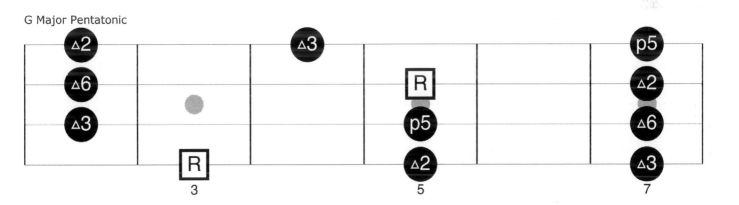

Then, over the C7, use the following shape. It's identical to the pentatonic shape we saw in Example 2i with the addition of one note, the b7. This is a fantastic shape to use over a dominant chord.

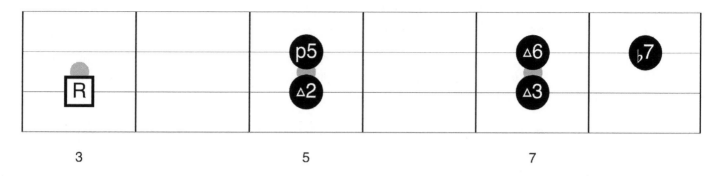

You can fret most of the notes with your first and third fingers, which will also take care of the slides and bends. I suggest following the indicated fingerings, shifting your hand quickly when required.

The tricky part is in the last bar. Slide into the 7th fret from the 5th, using your third finger. Then you can use your second and third fingers to bend and release the note on the 7th fret of the D string. Listen to the audio for clarification.

Example 2x

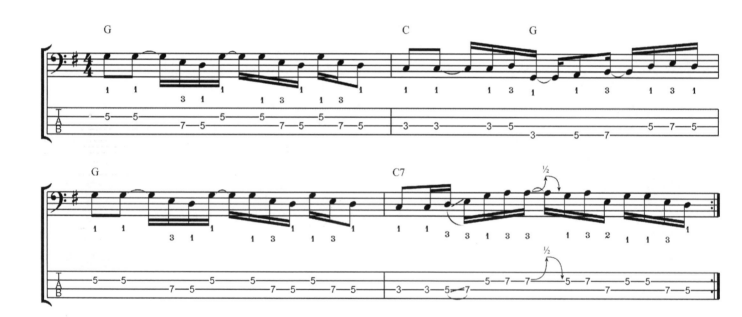

The first bar of the next example outlines the notes of the G7 chord with the G7 arpeggio below.

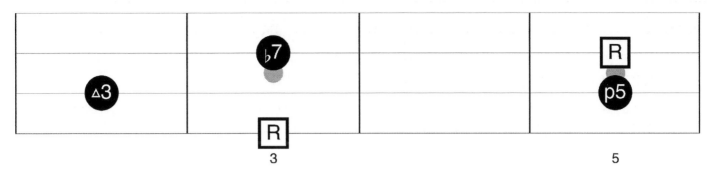

Listen to how a theoretical concept like an arpeggio can be brought to life by using interesting rhythms and take this approach when it comes to creating your own lines and fills. Take the shape above and get creative with a few simple rhythms using only those notes.

Cogbill used to love spelling out the chord changes using chord tones, much as a jazz soloist would. It shows how the bass can morph between rhythmic, harmonic and melodic roles. It's an incredibly important role and one in which Soul bass players were especially proficient.

When playing the next example, use the open E note to quickly shift into first position then back to start the riff again on the repeat.

Example 2y

Chapter Three – Motown

Motown Records was formed by Berry Gordy in 1960 in Detroit. The name Motown is a portmanteau of *motor* and *town*, reflecting the working-class roots of the *Motor City*. Such was the popularity of the label that Motown became its own sub-genre of Soul music that is known the world over.

Motown was the most successful of all the Soul music record labels, having nearly eighty records in the Billboard Hot 100 in the 1960s and tens of millions of sales.

Gordy's genius was to surround himself with musicians who could create a commercial sound in no time at all. He achieved this by assembling the greatest house band of all – the Funk Brothers – and having them record sessions at Hitsville U.S.A. This production line was made possible only by the talented musicians who recorded day in day out, reading off chord charts and creating memorable parts.

Such was the lack of credit given to these session superstars that they rode the Motown wave yet were largely unknown musicians in a hugely successful era. That would change in later years as the Funk Brothers found their deserved credit in books and documentaries (check out *Standing in the Shadows of Motown*).

The main bass player for the Funk Brothers was the peerless James Jamerson. Many people call him the greatest bass player of all time and it's hard to disagree with this statement. He was an undisputed genius who influenced scores of bass players, many of whom never knew he was playing those glorious improvised basslines.

The Motown songwriters would sometimes write parts for him that just didn't work, and his magic often came from the total creative freedom he applied, armed with just a chord chart, his ears, his instincts and imagination.

Jamerson was a jazz upright bass player who transitioned to electric as more work called for the new sound. With a high action on his bass, an unusual one-fingered plucking technique, and the skills of a top-class jazz man, Jamerson effortlessly crafted basslines at the click of a finger.

Bob Babbitt was the other bass player for Motown, who could hold his own with Jamerson. His involvement with the Funk Brothers increased in the late '60s due to Jamerson's tragic battles with alcoholism. In total, Babbitt played on over two hundred American Top 40 hit recordings for artists like Stevie Wonder, Marvin Gaye and Diana Ross.

His tone was clear and fat and his groove immense. Similar to Donald "Duck" Dunn, Babbitt was adept at creating memorable parts that were integral to a song's success.

Gear Checklist

Jamerson's weapon of choice was a 1962 Fender Precision dubbed The Funk Machine. This bass replaced two other Precisions that were stolen and he used heavy gauge LaBella flatwound strings that he rarely changed. A large part of his sound came from plucking with one finger on these strings, coupled with a high action. The bridge cover on his bass contained a foam mute which simulated the tone of a double bass. That made sense, as many players of the time were transitioning from the double bass to a Fender bass.

Jamerson used an Ampeg B15 on live dates but his trademark tone came from plugging directly into the Motown studio desk and using the signal to drive the board and create a mildly overdriven, naturally compressed tone that sat beautifully in any mix.

In later years, Babbitt favoured Phil Jones amplification and various modern basses, but at heart he was a four-string Fender guy. By the late '60s he was playing a 1968 Fender Precision but most of his Motown recordings sound like the tried-and-tested Precision with flatwound strings formula.

Recommended Listening

What's Going On – Marvin Gaye

Darling Dear – The Jackson 5

Home Cookin' – Jr. Walker & The All Stars

Signed, Sealed, Delivered, I'm Yours – Stevie Wonder

The Tears of A Clown – Smokey Robinson & The Miracles

Mercy Mercy Me (The Ecology) – Marvin Gaye

James Jamerson

Jamerson said that a bassline needed to sing like a voice and no line encapsulates this ideal better than Marvin Gaye's *What's Going On*. These first five examples are written in a similar melodic style and played in the key of A Major. They all fit together, so experiment by playing them one after the other or changing their order.

In Example 3a, the rhythms are syncopated throughout, so you may find it useful to listen to the audio example. Use your third or fourth fingers for notes on the 4th fret, then either use the same finger to *roll* to the same fret on the next string down or use a different finger to fret it.

Notice the chromatic notes used to connect chords that Jamerson often played and how they contribute to the flowing, connected nature of this bassline.

Example 3a

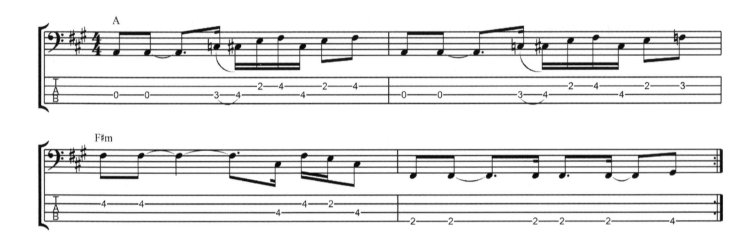

Jamerson's improvised basslines often didn't repeat the same thing twice – an influence from his jazz background. The next example uses the same chord progression and alters the bassline pattern, showing how to create real fluidity in your lines.

Watch out for the hammer-on in bar one, then use *raking* in the second bar. This is a technique Jamerson used often that involves plucking with one finger across different strings (usually high to low). Use your index finger to rake the A, E and C# in bar two.

Example 3b

The next example goes to the ii and V chords in A Major (Bm7 and E7). Once again, it makes sense to rake the first three notes of bar two. Concentrate on the timing of the release of your fretting hand fingers and isolate those three notes, cycling them round until you get them under control.

Example 3c

Jamerson would often outline the harmony using seventh arpeggios and notes from the key's home scale. Using the same chord progression as the previous example, let's explore this idea further. The first bar of each chord spells out the chord tones, then the next bar uses some scale notes to inject some melody.

Study the diagrams below, then experiment with them to construct your own lines in a similar style. Jamerson loved syncopated 1/16th note rhythms, so add some in.

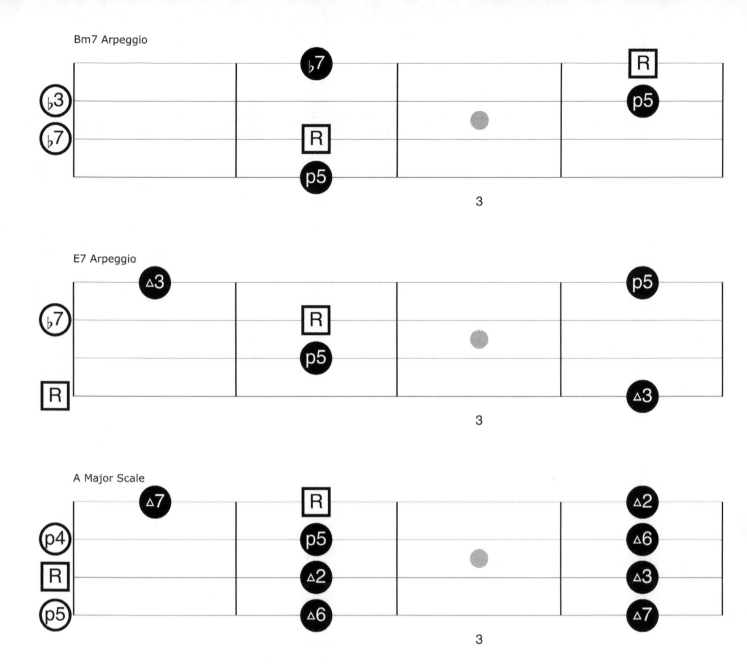

Great basslines are all about the alchemy of chord tones, scale tones, rhythms and phrasing (which involves articulations and expressive techniques). It sounds simple but it takes work to get it all under your fingers!

Example 3d

While Jamerson loved to use open strings (another favourite double bass technique), he also used roots and 5ths a lot, and there are two basic patterns to memorise. The first is *ascending* from the root to the 5th, the second is *descending* from the root to the 5th. The moveable pattern is summarised by these two diagrams that combine root, 5th and octave.

Root 5th pattern - closed position (B)

Root 5th pattern - open position (A)

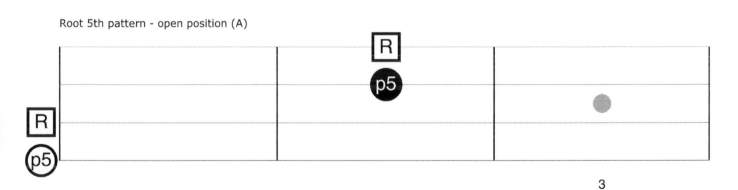

The next example demonstrates how effective just roots and 5ths can be in bassline construction. Either play notes on adjacent strings with the same finger with the rolling technique or use two different fingers. However, using raking in conjunction with rolling will make these types of rhythms easier to play.

Once you have this line down, use the diagrams above to shift to the different chord roots and make up your own lines.

Example 3e

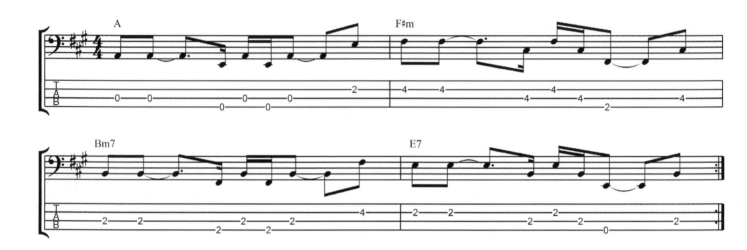

The next example uses chromaticism and notes from the E Major scale to lead strongly into each chord. Use your first finger to play the notes on the 2nd fret and the third or fourth finger for the 4th fret. Even if you don't read music, I encourage you to study reading 1/16th note rhythms. If you look closely, you'll see the same rhythms cropping up all the time in this style. Keep your foot tapping on the beats while you subdivide each one into 1/16ths.

Some people like to count "one e and a two e and a three e and a four e and a". I like to keep "da-ga-da-ga" going through my head on each beat. Either way, it locks you into a 1/16th note grid and eventually the feel becomes entirely natural. Stick with it.

Example 3f

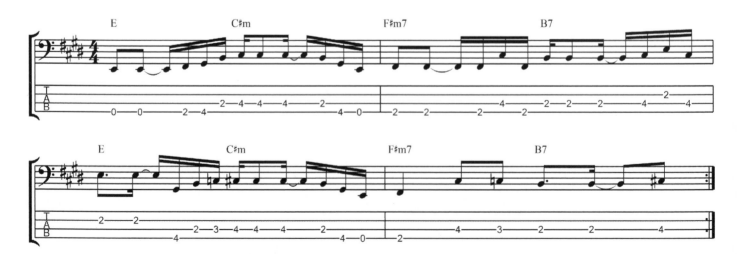

Jamerson didn't only play improvised basslines. Sometimes a Duck Dunn-inspired hook was the order of the day as heard in *Uptight (Everything's Alright)* and *(Your Love Keeps Lifting Me) Higher & Higher*. The next few examples are in this style.

Example 3g contains no 1/16th notes but you still need to count in 1/8ths as many of the notes are played on the offbeat.

Example 3g

Example 3h uses notes from E Major along with chromatics to anticipate each chord. You don't need to shift at all and can use your first and fourth (or third) fingers to fret throughout.

Example 3h

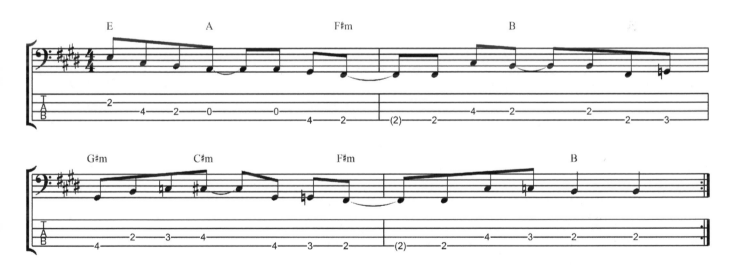

By the time you've played through the basslines in this book and listened to the Spotify playlist, you'll begin to recognise Soul basslines in other styles of music. For example, listen to The B-52's *Love Shack* and you'll hear Jamerson's influence. This next example is in a similar style and sticks to the riff-based approach of the previous two lines.

In the first bar, use your first finger to mute the open A string as it comes down to fret the F# to stop the A from ringing out.

Example 3i

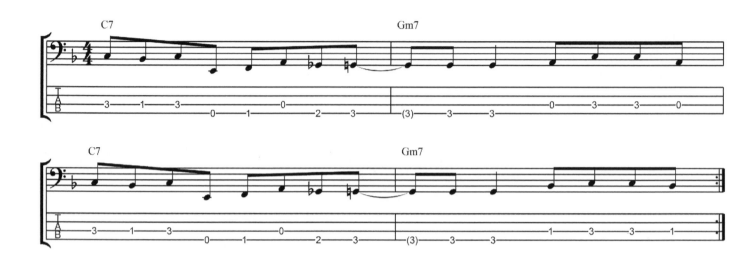

Jamerson's lines were one-part bass, one-part percussion. He would build his lines around intricate drum rhythms and create incredible grooves, the likes of which no one had heard before. You can definitely hear his influence in players like Bootsy Collins and Rocco Prestia.

The next example uses the open E string to bounce around a chromatic pattern and Jamerson would often use open strings in this way. Use alternate plucking and raking where appropriate to get this line together. It's incredible to think that Jamerson would play this kind of thing plucking with just one finger!

Go through the example beat by beat while listening to the audio.

Example 3j

For a bassline that contains every Jamerson trick in the book, listen to JR Walker's *Home Cookin'*. The next example uses that kind of syncopation and a busy chromatic line with some articulations to recreate the feel. Jamerson normally improvised during recording sessions using his prodigious sense of rhythm and harmony, so it's easy to get overwhelmed when reading lines like this.

Take this example beat by beat and focus on getting the line up to half speed. It will soon come together after that. Use your second and third fingers for the hammer-ons in bars one and two and watch out for the 1/16th note rest in the last bar. You can play the ghost note in a variety of places but try it on the 4th fret of the A string as that's the note you end up on.

Example 3k

Jamerson not only explored arpeggio notes, but also how to use notes to lead into the next chord. This sometimes required the kind of shifting seen in the next example.

Start in first position (with your first finger lining up at the 1st fret) then shift your hand up one fret during the open A to bring you into the correct position to play the F#. Next, use the open G to shift back into first position before using raking the first three notes of the last bar.

Example 3l

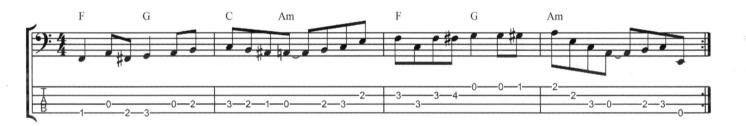

The next example features swing 1/8ths and uses a Ray Brown-inspired rhythmic skip to add interest and forward motion to a simple walking bassline. Listen to Martha and the Vandellas' *Heatwave* for a good example of this style of playing.

To play the skip, rake the first two notes with your middle finger, then pluck the open D with your index before following through with the same finger to rake the A string. Isolate those four notes and practice slowly until you get it right.

A good way to build speed (and timing) is to set a metronome to a comfortable speed, then build from there in 5bpm intervals per practice session. Another excellent thing to do is to half the metronome speed and feel it as beats two and four, to simulate the *backbeat* of the snare drum. If you incorporate these timing exercises into your routine, you'll quickly develop your groove and feel.

Example 3m

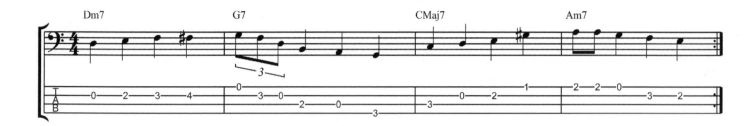

Like Tommy Cogbill, James Jamerson could get busy without distracting from the song. Often in pop, busy simply means "playing too much" and bass parts are often whittled down to their most basic form. Not so with Jamerson. This next bassline is an example of busy playing where the rhythm and note choice enhance the track.

Remain in first position until the transition from bar three to four. Shift your hand across at that point, so you can rake a finger across the strings for the first three notes in bar four. Then, shift back during the tied G. It's those ties that create the lilting syncopated feel of this bassline.

Make sure to tap your foot firmly on the beats, so that you can clearly mark exactly where the notes to play lie. Keep subdividing the bar when you count.

The next two examples are in the same key and tempo so can be played together. There's a backing track for the next example that combines the two chord progressions.

Example 3n

No open strings are used in the next example. Follow the notation then figure out what shapes (that we've encountered before) are being used by moving the open string note to a fretted note on the lower string. Seeing how open strings can be used instead of fretted notes will help you craft your own basslines as well as memorise lines effortlessly by using patterns.

Shift to the G in the second bar with your first finger before shifting back to the Bb at the first fret. The remainder of the line can be played in the same position.

Example 3o

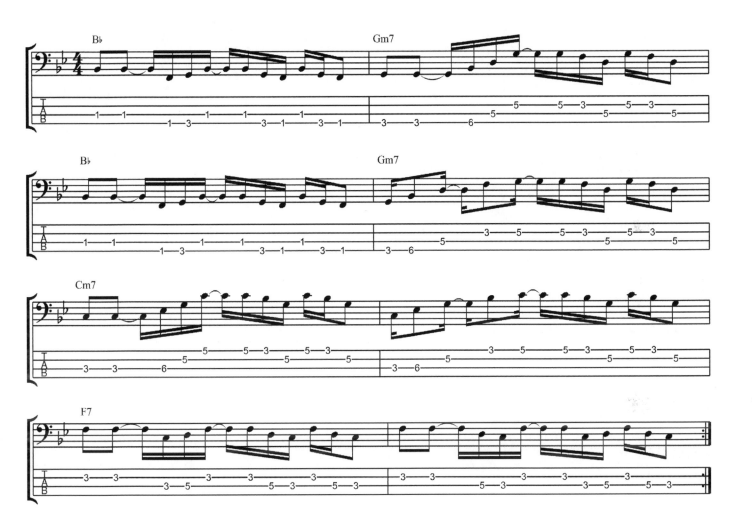

Bob Babbitt

Babbitt always crafted strong bass parts that outlined the harmony and often used repetitive rhythms as illustrated in the following example. This whole line can be played down in first position but make sure you move your finger quickly from the last G back to the C on the A string.

Example 3p

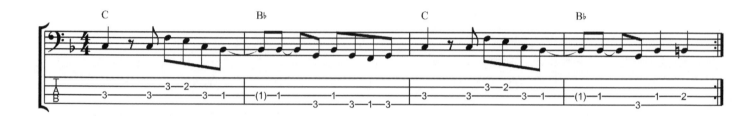

Example 3q uses the G Minor Pentatonic scale to create an interesting riff over the static Gm chord. Use the shape below to create similar lines over the backing track. The notes of a Gm7 arpeggio are indicated by the hollow circles. Those are particularly strong notes as they make up the chord. Any of the notes from the scale will sound great.

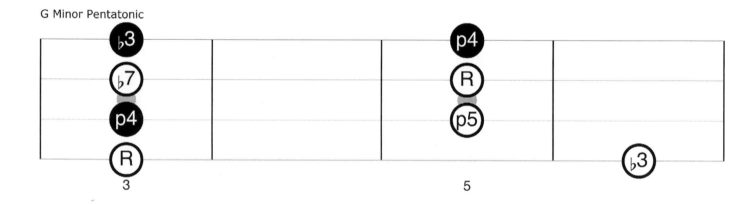

Example 3q

Marvin Gaye's *Mercy Mercy Me (The Ecology)* is a beautiful example of a repeating rhythm over a set of chord changes. Here, Babbitt plays simple notes over the chords and sticks to a reassuring rhythm. Compare this to Jamerson's style of rarely playing the same thing twice!

If you like, you can play the 5th fret notes on open strings but, in my opinion, you get far more control by fretting them.

Example 3r

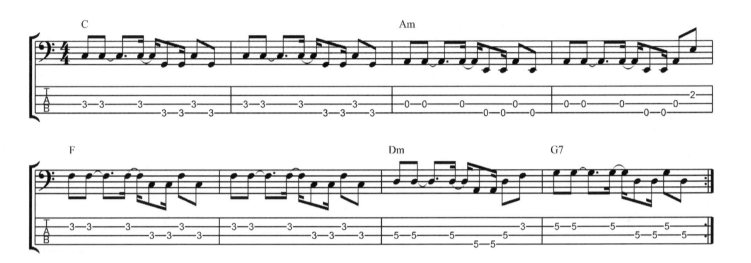

Motown is often characterised by pulsating bass rhythms, even in slower songs. In this example, the bassline is more relaxed but includes some 1/16th note rhythms to create forward motion.

Hold the dotted 1/4 notes for their full length and subdivide the beats into 1/16ths when you get to them. The goal is for your counting and playing to become one. The strong sense of rhythm forged by working on your internal clock will make your playing sound more professional and musical.

Regular playing with a metronome, backing tracks and drum loops, and ideally a band, will help you develop your sense of time.

Example 3s

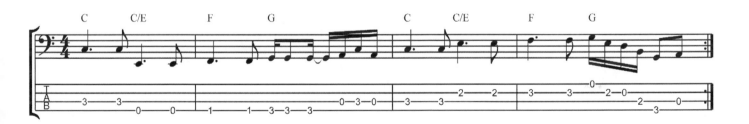

In the next example a descending E minor arpeggio outlines the chord. If you play an interesting rhythm, even simple chord tones don't sound boring! There are lots of ties and notes played on the offbeat so tap your foot confidently, syncing any offbeat notes (the ones after the 1/8th note rests) with your foot coming up off the floor.

Example 3t

Chapter Four – West Coast Motown

Berry Gordy established Motown offices in LA in the early 1960s and eventually moved all of the operations out West in 1972. This created a big change in the musicians and writing teams, with some artists initially staying in Detroit, such as the members of the Funk Brothers.

Yet, the West coast operation didn't have the unity of sound and image of Detroit and couldn't match the success of the early Motown years. Motown aficionados may turn their noses up at some of the output during this period, but still many classics were created along the way.

The sound and the teams may have changed but the Motown machine rolled on for a few more years before being overtaken by Disco, Funk and Rock.

The three bassists featured in this chapter were among a coterie of players called upon by the various Motown teams.

Wilton Felder was the main Motown bass player when they moved to LA. He played saxophone and bass, coming to prominence as a founder member of the commercially successful multi-genre group The Crusaders. They peaked with their smash hit *Street Life*, but Felder was to be immortalised by his low-end involvement with several smash hits. He had a melodic, lyrical style, probably stemming from his song writing and sax skills.

One of the more bizarre episodes in bass folklore must be the clash between Carole Kaye's controversial Motown credit claims and James Jamerson's fans and peers. It is beyond the scope of this book to even go there, but it does seem that Kaye did in fact play on a fair few Motown originals, not just the Broadway and cover versions she definitely played on… allegedly!

I hope you'll forgive this quick name drop, but years ago I played many gigs with Martha Reeves and the Vandellas. One of my favourite basslines to play was *I'm Ready for Love* and it took me years to discover that it was Kaye and not Jamerson who came up with and recorded the part.

Her place in history as one of the most recorded session players (as part of the Wrecking Crew) is without question. She deserves credit for her involvement with Motown, even if James Jamerson will always be the star of that particular show.

Scott Edwards is probably the least known musician in this book, but he makes up for it with his wonderfully creative lines and muscular tone. He gave up a scholarship as a physics major to pursue his lifelong dream of becoming a Motown bass player, which he fulfilled when he joined Stevie Wonder's road band.

Such was the way of the Motown production machine. He didn't get to record much with Wonder, although he did play on *You Are the Sunshine of My Life* and *All in Love is Fair*.

Gear Checklist

Wilton Felder played a Fender Telecaster bass which was introduced in the late '60s and discontinued a decade later. It had a warm, old school tone due to being a single pickup version. You can search on YouTube for the isolated bass to *I Want You Back* to hear it in action.

Carole Kaye was famous for her use of a plectrum which you can clearly hear on Martha and the Vandellas' *I'm Ready for Love*. She would often record with a Fender amp. Earlier in her career, that would be the only signal recorded but, later on, it would be half amp, half DI. She used flatwound strings and a felt mute on top of the strings at the bridge.

Being a James Jamerson disciple, Scott Edwards was a P bass guy. I recommend checking out his back catalogue, because where Jamerson struggled with the demands of the post-Motown era, Edwards thrived in a multitude of different musical styles (he played on *I Will Survive*, *Hot Stuff* and some of the *Saturday Night Fever* album).

Recommended Listening

I Want You Back – The Jackson 5

ABC – The Jackson 5

Let's Get It On – Marvin Gaye

I'm Ready for Love – Martha Reeves & The Vandellas

Love Is Here and Now You're Gone – The Supremes

Someday We'll Be Together – Diana Ross & The Supremes

Being With You – Smokey Robinson

You Are the Sunshine of My Life – Stevie Wonder

Love Machine – The Miracles

Wilton Felder

Example 4a should be played with an easy, relaxed feel. Tap your foot and keep your breathing regular as this will help you keep in time. Many people tense up when they play, causing their breath to shorten and their playing to suffer. Good players relax, so try that out on this line!

Example 4a

The next two examples can be played together and are in the style of The Jackson Five's *I Want You Back,* which features chromatic notes and plenty of rhythm. I recommend taking this one bar by bar and studying the audio example closely.

Wherever you see a 1/16th note rest, the following note is always the second 1/16th note of the bar, which can be a tough one to place. Tap your foot slowly while subdividing the beat into four separate 1/16ths. Take your time feeling where that tricky second note lies. Do this slowly then build up the speed once you've sussed it out. Watch out for the quick shift at the end of bar three.

Example 4b

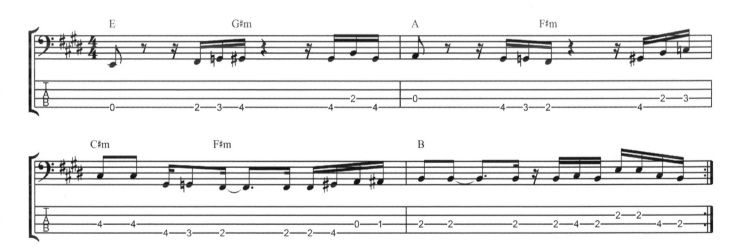

The next example uses the same chord progression but has more of a driving feel, with more 1/8th notes. Use alternate plucking throughout and once you get this line down, run it together with the previous example.

Example 4c

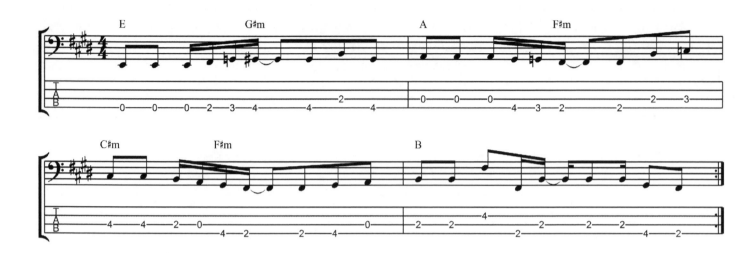

Example 4d features swing 1/16th notes so listen to the audio to catch the rhythm if you're unsure. Once you can feel them, make sure to subdivide each beat into swing 1/16ths. That will make it much easier to play the groove properly, and especially to catch the C at the end of beat two.

Example 4d

All the notes in the next example are in a closed position, with no open strings being used, and will require some hand shifts. Look out especially for bar one where you go to the C. The benefit of this approach is that you can use the same patterns over the Am and Bm chords (the root, 5, b7 and octave). Using patterns to help you memorise basslines, and seeing the lines like this, makes transposing to different keys much easier.

Example 4e

Carole Kaye

Martha and the Vandellas' *I'm Ready for Love* is a riff-based line that mirrors the horn rhythms. The first example uses a similar approach, with mostly roots, 5ths and octaves to create a pulsating bassline.

This line is quite fast and consists of swing 1/8ths, so be sure to count those as you tap your foot. The first four bars use plenty of open strings, so you will need to mute with your fretting hand. Have your fingers straighter than you normally would when fretting and lightly touch them against the strings when you want the note to stop. Take your time with this and get used to the coordination required between the two hands.

Play any of these basslines with a plectrum to get the authentic Carole Kaye sound.

Example 4f

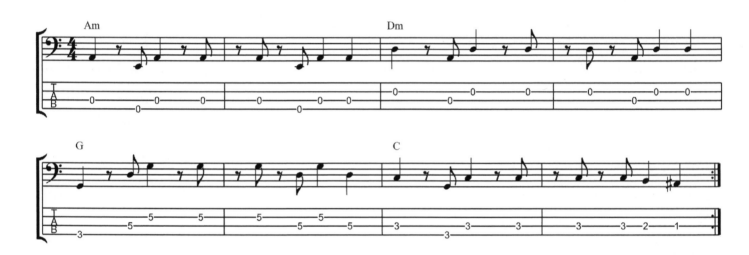

Kaye loved to use repeating rhythms as a hook, anchoring the arrangement while outlining the changes with simple chord tones. The next example is in the key of C Major and the rhythm remains the same throughout. Once you've learned the line, use the diagram below to embellish the bassline.

Here are some techniques for you to try:

- Match the notes in the diagram to the root notes of the chord symbols (above the TAB/notation)

- Use the notes from the scale to connect the chords in a musical way

- Play the notes in different places than in the notation

- Use some of the patterns you've learned in this book

- Play a fill in the last bar by ascending or descending the scale until you hit the C on the repeat

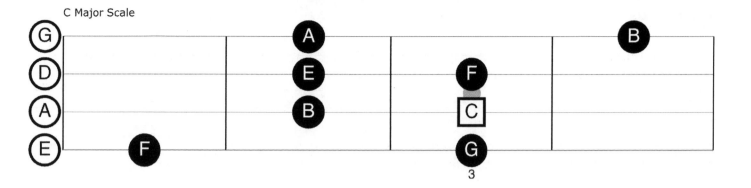

C Major Scale

Example 4g

As a session player, Kaye was required to be a musical chameleon and was comfortable in a huge range of styles.

Example 4h is a funky Soul line built from the root, 5th, b7 and octave of the Cm7 chord. You can play the entire line in one position but make sure to pluck alternately to execute the fast 1/16th note runs.

Example 4h

Now let's take the same pattern and move it to different roots. Watch out for the hand shifts between the Cm7 and Bbm7 chords, and on the repeat. You can use the backing track to practice them. After a while, you can change up some of the rhythms and even the order of the notes.

Example 4i

The next example is in the key of G Major and can be played in one position. Line up your first finger over the 1st fret and use your second finger to play any notes on the 2nd fret. Use you third or fourth to play notes on the 3rd fret. That way, you don't need to shift position.

Of course, if you want to play in second position with your first finger at the 2nd fret and shift to play the D#, feel free to do so.

Example 4j

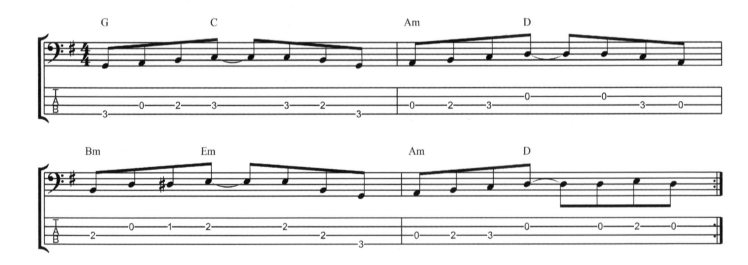

Scott Edwards

You can play the following three examples together as they're all in the key of C Major.

Example 4k uses the Major Pentatonic scale in a closed position (see below) to help introduce some slides. Start with your first finger, then slide into the 7th fret from two frets below. Use your third or fourth finger for the slide then shift back quickly from the 5th to 3rd at the end of the phrase.

The patterns are the same for each chord and create a classic sound often used by the early Soul players. You can use it over any major chord.

C Major Penatatonic (moveable shape)

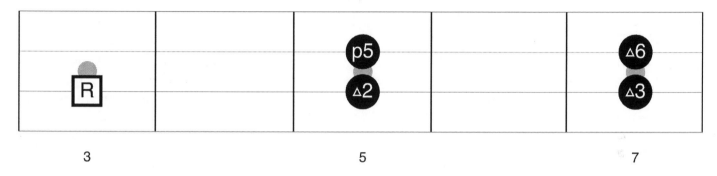

Example 4k

This next example is built around another beautiful pentatonic shape.

C Major Penatatonic (moveable shape)

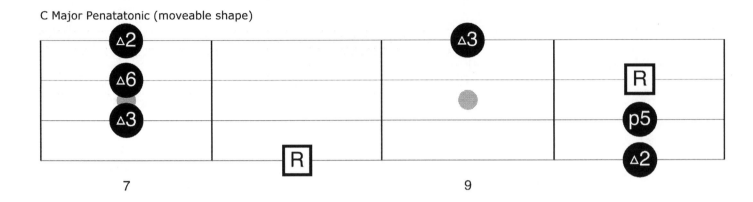

Notice how the entire line is created from the shape above. The notes of the pentatonic scale are particularly melodic and you'll hear them a lot in all types of basslines. Pay close attention to the fill in the last bar and then use the shape above and the backing track to create your own fills. Everything can be played in seventh position without shifting your hand.

Example 4l

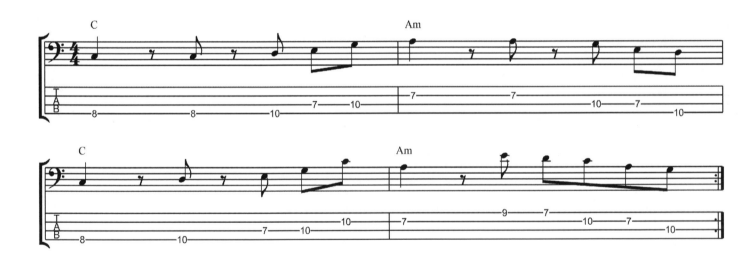

Edwards loved to use articulations and he was extremely influential in the later Disco and Funk genres where articulations feature heavily in the basslines. These expressive techniques include hammer-ons, pull-offs, bends, slides, vibrato and ghost notes.

Articulations aren't something you hear a huge amount in Soul bass playing but they can be effective. The next example uses slides; specifically, sliding into a note from two frets below. For both slides, using your third finger keeps your first finger in position, ready and waiting to play the next note. Play through it slowly then build up speed while connecting all the notes smoothly.

Example 4m

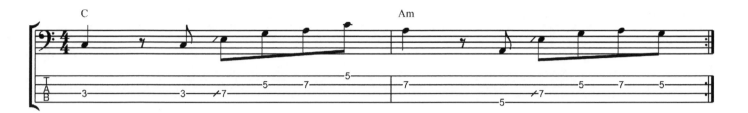

Love Machine was a huge Motown hit for The Miracles. The following two examples are a nod to the more upbeat, funky hits that were being recorded in the mid 1970s. Edwards borrowed Jamerson's use of chromatics and Example 4n does the same in the last bar to outline an Em chord.

The following diagram shows the notes of the Em arpeggio (hollow circles) and the chromatic notes leading to the chord tones.

Em chord tones (E,G,B,E) with chromatic passing notes

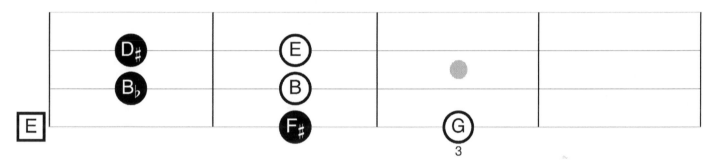

Mute the open E string so it doesn't ring out beyond its value of half a beat.

Example 4n

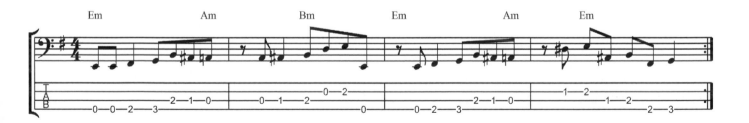

The next example gives you more practice at dampening open strings. It also features lots of notes on the second half of the beat, so keep your foot tapping and watch out for the upbeats.

Example 4o

Chapter Five – Philly Soul

In the late 1960s, Funk was starting to take hold. However, Soul was still in full force and the music coming from Philadelphia blended the two styles, especially in the latter part of the 1970s.

Just as Motown had the Funk Brothers, assembled by Berry Gordy, Philadelphia had its own secret weapon: MFSB ("Mother Father Sister Brother") who were the house band at Sigma Sound Studios. They were put together by super-producers Gamble and Huff and were able to create a sound in the same way that Motown did. This stardust was sprinkled over acts that passed through the studio including The Spinners, Wilson Pickett and The O'Jays.

The main bass player in MFSB was the titanic Ronnie Baker, one of the most underrated bass players of all time. It's extraordinary how little is known about him in the wider bass community, considering how many incredible basslines he created on a plethora of hits including the Disco hits *Love Train, Disco Inferno, I'll Be Around* and *Bad Luck*. His anonymity was partly down to the label's inadequacy in crediting the musicians who helped craft the hit records.

His style was groovy and supportive, often locking in closely with Earl Young's kick drum and holding back on the flashy fills. This left space for the lush string and horn arrangements that made up the Sound of Philadelphia.

When Baker left, Jimmie Williams joined Philadelphia International Records. He is perhaps best known for his line on McFadden & Whitehead's *Ain't No Stoppin' Us Now*, and his long-time stint for The O'Jays. His playing was precise and dexterous, and he would create repetitive parts that acted as a song's hook.

It's interesting to parallel Williams' ascent into Funk bass playing and beyond with Jamerson, who was reluctant to play a different style to the one he became famous for. Just like Scott Edwards, however, Jimmie adapted and thrived.

Gear Checklist

You can hear the influence of James Jamerson on Ronnie Baker's tone and style, especially on *Bad Luck* by Harold Melvin & The Blue Notes. Like Jamerson, Baker used a Fender Precision strung with heavy gauge flatwound strings played through an Ampeg B15. He loved old, dead strings and it's been said that he covered his Fender heavy gauge flatwounds with butter for a year before putting them on the bass. That story sounds highly dubious to me and I wouldn't recommend it!

Jimmie Williams tone was punchy and upfront in the mix. This was partly down to technique and partly due to the production and mixing techniques of the time. He played a Yamaha bass later in his career, but it sounds like he used a Fender Precision with flats during the Philly Soul years.

Recommended Listening

Bad Luck – Harold Melvin & The Blue Notes

I'll Be Around – The Spinners

The Horse – Cliff Nobles

Love TKO – Teddy Pendergrass

Close the Door – Teddy Pendergrass

Your Body's Here with Me – The O'Jays

Ronnie Baker

The first example is a I iii IV V progression in the key of C Major (C, Em, F, G). Keep the 1/8th notes nice and steady and try not to rush the 1/16ths. Always use alternate plucking and isolate the fast sections, working them up to speed with a metronome.

Example 5a

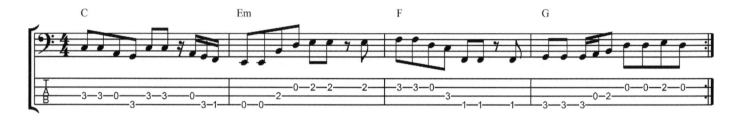

Baker was a master of creating memorable lines over two chords, such as the one on The Spinners' *I'll Be Around*. Example 5b takes a IV V progression in the key of C (F to G) and uses chord and scale tones to create melodic interest in the bassline while anchoring the groove and outlining the harmony.

Example 5b

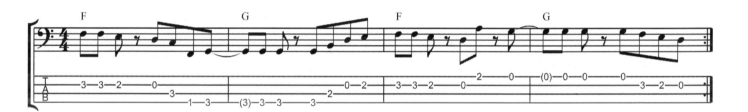

The next example adds a trademark flourish at the end of the line. Use the second finger for the hammer-on and to play all notes on the 2nd fret. Rake the final two notes by plucking the G string with your index finger then follow through in the same direction to pluck the D string too, eventually coming to rest on the A string.

Example 5c

Example 5d uses the same chords but reverses them for a faster tempo line, so you'll need to work this one up to speed slowly. Follow the TAB closely and start in fifth position, with your first finger lined up at the 5th fret

As you play the ghost note, shift your hand so that your third finger plays the D on the 5th fret and your first finger is in position to play the next G. It doesn't matter where you play a ghost note as long as you create a dead, percussive sound.

Example 5d

There's a backing track to play along to for the next example, which is a ii V vamp in the key of G Major (Am7 to D7). Although there are many 1/16th notes in this line, the tempo is quite slow. Even so, don't rush the hammer-ons at the end of bar two.

Example 5e

Jimmie Williams

This first example highlights Jimmie Williams' up-front, punchy style. It's played at 80bpm, so the 1/16th notes aren't hard to play. Use the backing track for practice.

Example 5f

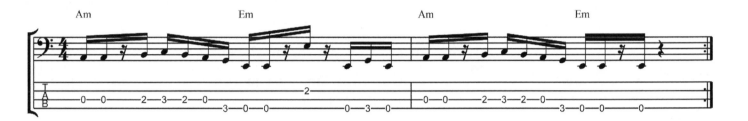

Let's take the same bassline and add a bit of Soul with some articulations. This example adds a slide and a hammer-on to the previous line. Slide into the E on the 7th fret with your fourth finger then shift quickly back into position. Sliding in from the 5th fret will sound good.

In the next bar, use the open E to shift quickly to the 5th fret for the hammer-on. Since the next note is an open string, you have time to shift back into position. Using rests, ghost notes and open strings makes shifting easier and subsequently brings a smoother sound to your playing.

Example 5g

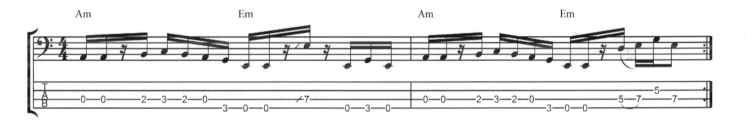

Williams knew how to open up and let fly (check out McFadden & Whitehead's *Ain't No Stoppin' Us Now*) but he was also the king of the understated, supportive bassline.

Feel is one of the most important concepts for a bass player to grasp. There is a big difference between a master bassist playing a simple line and someone who has no idea about feel playing the same thing. Having excellent timing, a strong appreciation of note length, and control over where you place the beat will develop your feel. A bassist with great time and feel is a valuable one indeed.

Count "**1** e and a **2** e and a **3** e and a **4** e and a" through the line. It's the notes that land on the "a" (the fourth 1/16th in the beat) that you need to watch out for. Take it slow and work daily on this until you gain control over counting and 1/16th note placement.

Example 5h

Here's the same bassline with some extra notes. Use the backing track to lock into the line and listen to the audio example for inspiration. Use these two examples to hone your counting and rhythmic skills.

Example 5i

The next bassline requires a couple of hand shifts. Start at the 3rd fret with your first finger, then shift so that your fourth plays the second C in bar two (taking over from the first finger). You're then in position for the next few notes. Shift back up again for bar three, then make one last quick shift to the Bb on the 1st fret. This line is a little nod to the Disco lines that were influenced by Williams, Baker and the Philly sound.

Example 5j

Chapter Six – Atlantic and Muscle Shoals

Two more hotbeds of Soul music were found in New York City's Atlantic Records and FAME studios based in Muscle Shoals, Alabama.

Atlantic turned Aretha Franklin into the Queen of Soul with many fine bass players recording for her. One of them, Jerry Jemmott, features in this chapter, although there were countless others.

That's the thing about Soul music in the '60s. Players like Tommy Cogbill, a Memphis Boy, would be flown around the country to record. Producers knew the importance of master musicians and would want the best on their records. In fact, Atlantic producer Jerry Wexler brought Aretha down to Muscle Shoals for her first session. Just like in Detroit with The Funk Brothers, the formula for success was associated with specific places and groups of musicians.

One such player was David Hood, who was best known for his work with the Muscle Shoals Sound Studio in Sheffield, Alabama. He was part of a house band known as The Muscle Shoals Rhythm Section. They were also known as The Swampers (they're referred to in the song *Sweet Home Alabama*) and included Barry Beckett on keys, drummer Roger Hawkins and guitarist Jimmy Johnson.

The Muscle Shoals relaxed vibe blended southern music styles, Country, RnB and Soul. It led to an unmistakable groove which backed many a hit including Wilson Pickett's *Mustang Sally* and The Staple Singers' *I'll Take You There*. The musicians rarely read music, instead coming up with their own parts much like The Funk Brothers. This creative approach released them from the shackles that some of the Atlantic sessions musicians had with their often written parts.

Jerry Jemmott grew up in NYC and became one of the prominent session bassists of the late '60s and early '70s. King Curtis discovered him and it was Jemmott who played on the live version of Memphis Soul Stew, nailing Tommy Cogbill's famous bassline. King Curtis was signed to Atlantic and it was through this connection that Jemmott played on many sessions for the label.

Along with Cogbill, Jerry Jemmott was a big influence on Jaco Pastorius. You can hear why when you hear his playing on songs like Nina Simone's *Ain't Got No, I Got Life* with his use of relentless 1/16th note lines.

Gear Checklist

In a rare departure from the P bass monopoly, David Hood used a Fender Jazz. His first was a 1961 model but, in keeping with many of the players featured in this book, it was stolen! Later, he used an Alembic and then various Lakland models.

While Hood used the studio's Fender Bassman amp, he said the tone is, "more in the bass and my hands". The amp was an original with a 2x12 speaker cabinet which would sometimes be captured via a microphone, but often his signal would go direct to the mixing desk.

Jerry Jemmott was another Fender Jazz player, usually stringing his '65 and '69 models with flatwounds. He used the ubiquitous Ampeg B15 on many of his Soul recordings.

Recommended Listening

I'll Take You There – The Staple Singers

Mustang Sally – Wilson Pickett

Respect yourself – The Staple Singers

Think – Aretha Franklin

Instant Groove – King Curtis

You Send Me – Aretha Franklin

David Hood

Example 6a uses the root, 5, b7 pattern to create a simple but effective line that provides a cool groove while outlining the C7 chord. Play the tied notes for their full duration, tapping your foot so that you can easily identify the next upbeat 1/8th note.

Example 6a

In a similar style to Duck Dunn, Hood liked to create simple but memorable repeating figures. There's no greater example than The Staple Singers' *I'll Take You There*.

There are a few ways to fret this line, so feel free to experiment till you find something comfortable. I recommend fretting the notes on the 3rd fret with your first finger. Fret the C on the A string roughly at the crease behind your first knuckle then roll your fingertip onto the G.

Be ready to shift quickly to the F on the D string.

Example 6b

Soul playing often takes place towards the low end of the bass with players rarely venturing to the "dusty end". However, Hood created at least two memorable higher register mini-solos in *I'll Take You There* and *Respect Yourself*.

Example 6c is in the key of A Minor and uses an upper register A Minor Blues scale. Here's a diagram for you to study so that you can try your own solo lines over the backing track. There are more notes in that position which I haven't included, but these few will sound great!

Em chord tones (E,G,B,E) with chromatic passing notes

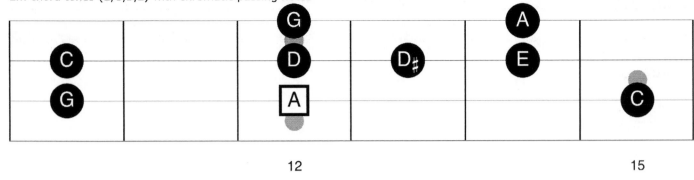

Use your first and third fingers to fret the notes and use hand shifts when you need to.

Example 6c

The Muscle Shoals sound included Country music in its melting pot of influences and the next example infuses some of that style. The rhythms are syncopated so you may find it helpful to listen to the audio example. Use your first and fourth fingers to fret, although you can use your third finger if you find it easier.

Example 6d

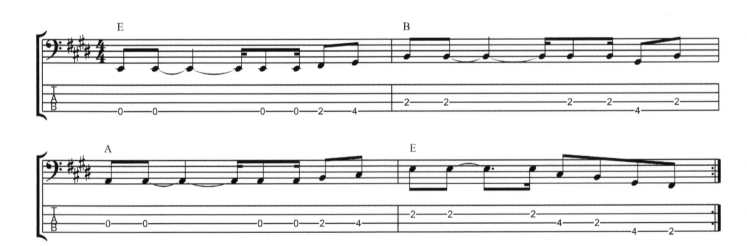

This example uses four chords in the key of A Minor (Am, G, F, Dm – a i VII VI iv chord progression). Hood and his contemporaries often outlined the chord changes by using notes from a chord's arpeggio.

Fret the 3rd fret notes with your third or fourth finger, so that you're in position for the F at the 1st fret. That way you can play the whole line without having to shift.

Example 6e

Jerry Jemmott

Due to his prodigious technique and dexterity on bass, Jemmott often leaned towards the funkier side of Soul. The notes in Example 6f should be played short and punchy, which you can achieve by controlling the fretting hand fingers. I find it easier to use my fourth finger on the 4th fret.

Example 6f

The following two examples can be played together as they're both in the same key and tempo. This line is a little like Jamerson's opening to *What's Going On* except it has more inflections and articulations. Use alternate plucking with as much precision and aggression as you can.

Slide into the second to last note with your third finger so that you're in position to start the groove again on the repeat.

Example 6g

The rhythms in the next example are syncopated, so listen to the audio example to hear how they go. It's much easier to keep your fretting hand in one position with the first finger taking care of the 2nd fret and the fourth (or third) finger playing notes on the 4th fret.

Notice the use of the chromatic notes that lead into chords. Once you have this line under your fingers, cycle between this and the previous example.

Example 6h

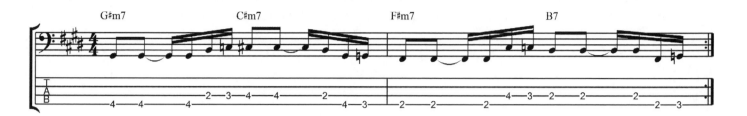

In his amazing bassline on Aretha Franklin's *Think*, Jemmott took a simple line and added a little rhythmic skip via a 1/16th note. The next example applies the same kind of idea around a simple I IV V chord progression in the key of C Major (C, F, G).

Keep all the notes full and connect them smoothly, except for the 1/16th notes which should be short and punchy to create an effective contrast. Look out for the ghost note in bar three as you need to be quick to release pressure on the 3rd fret before fretting again.

Example 6i

This idea of taking a simple chord progression and adding 1/16th notes works well in Soul basslines. The melodic passages in this line come from the key, which is C Major. Use your fourth finger for the notes on the 4th fret. Jam with the backing track and use the diagram below to practice your own lines.

Try to target the root of the chord then use notes from the scale and chromatics to connect the roots smoothly.

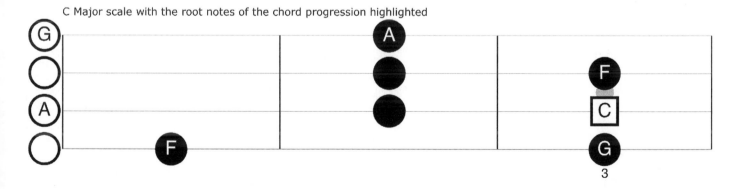

C Major scale with the root notes of the chord progression highlighted

Example 6j

Chapter Seven – Chicago Soul and Chess Records

As with Memphis, Chicago spawned a Soul scene that was influenced by Gospel music as well as RnB. Many of the emerging acts were vocal groups that the studios would hire to create new music, blending harmonies with horn and string arrangements and a killer rhythm section.

One of the big movers in the Windy City was guitarist, composer and lyricist Curtis Mayfield. He went on to become a big star in his own right after his stint with The Impressions. He also set up his own Curtom label which was one of many based in Chicago.

The legendary Soul singer Donny Hathaway was born in Chicago and worked for Curtom Records as a songwriter, producer and session musician. While not directly recorded in Chicago, *Voices Inside (Everything Is Everything)* features one of the greatest moments of bass playing by Willie Weeks. That incredible solo is the inspiration for his lines in this chapter.

Born in North Carolina, Willie Weeks went on to become a prolific session player in all manner of genres, working with everyone from Eric Clapton to Stevie Wonder. He's perhaps most famous for that bass solo which features on Donny Hathaway's live album – a must listen for any aspiring bass player.

Louis Satterfield is equally well known for his trombone work with Earth Wind & Fire and it's easy to make parallels with Wilton Felder who was also a horn player and master bass player. Satterfield was a prolific session player for Chess Records, one of Chicago's important studios at the time. He played for many of the Blues artists including B.B. King, Muddy Waters, Howling Wolf and Willie Dixon.

Chess was established in 1950 and was mainly a Blues and RnB label until it expanded into Soul. Satterfield played on many Soul hits coming out of Chicago, his most famous bassline being Fontella Bass' *Rescue Me*.

Gear Checklist

On *Donny Hathaway Live*, Willie Weeks played a 1962 Fender Precision with flatwound strings through an Ampeg SVT.

Louis Satterfield is one of the most unknown bass players, and there isn't much footage of him playing or of interviews with him. However, it does sound like he is playing a flatwound-strung P bass.

Recommended Listening

Voices Inside (Everything Is Everything) – Donny Hathaway (listen to the live version)

Papillon (aka Hot Butterfly) – Chaka Khan

He's Misstra Know-It-All – Stevie Wonder

Rescue Me – Fontella Bass

I Believe to My Soul – Donny Hathaway

Somebody's Been Sleeping – The Pharaohs

Louis Satterfield

Example 7a outlines the root, 5th and 6th of a G chord in a classic Soul pattern we saw earlier. Play the G on the 3rd fret with your first finger then shift quickly to the remaining notes. Feel free to figure this out using open strings, but the benefit of learning it this way is that you can move the pattern around to different roots.

Example 7a

Here's a reminder of the root, 5, major 6th pattern so common in Soul basslines.

Root, 5, Major 6th moveable pattern (G)

The next example takes the previous shape and moves it around different chords. These patterns work on all major chords so try them out when you're improvising. Use the same fingering pattern each time and focus on the quick hand shifts to help you land on beat one bang on time.

Example 7b

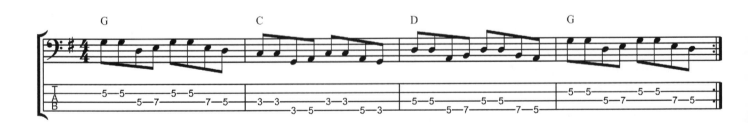

Satterfield had a wonderfully fluid playing style and would often weave hypnotically melodic lines over a chord. The next example uses notes from the A Minor Pentatonic scale and is a fantastic example of how to take a simple scale and bring it to life using good timing, feel, articulations and rhythms. Think of those elements as you use the backing track to improvise your own lines.

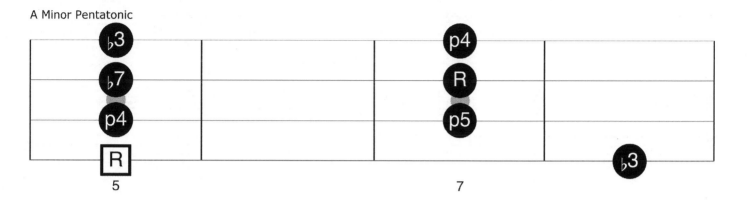

Play this line smoothly and be sure not to rush the pull-offs in bars 2-4. The tempo is quite slow so the 1/16ths aren't too fast.

Example 7c

The next example combines the previous two shapes at the same tempo. Once you feel comfortable with the line, use the backing track and the diagrams from the previous two examples to create your own lines.

Example 7d

Example 7e is a repetitive groove in the key of E Minor. Start out by using your first finger to fret the A on the 5th fret (instead of playing it open). Then, quickly shift your hand down two frets, bringing you into position for the remaining notes. Make sure the tied E is played for its full duration, then play the last two Es first short (*staccato*) then long.

Staccato is shown by the dot underneath the note. The dash under that next note is *tenuto* which means sustain the note for its full length. When you alter note lengths in this way, you can create interesting feels.

Example 7e

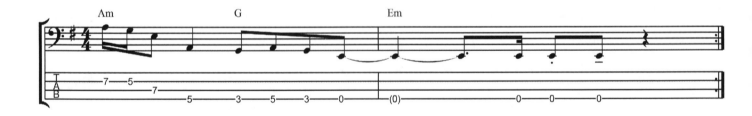

Willie Weeks

In Weeks' famous solo on the live version of *Voices Inside (Everything Is Everything)*, he uses a beautiful variety of Soul, RnB and Blues vocabulary, and the next examples combine these elements and are played with the bass more upfront in the mix.

With the ideas, shapes and patterns you'll learn here, you will quickly be able to create your own similar lines over the static E7 backing track. You can also combine all the examples in this chapter to work together over this backing track.

Example 7f starts off subdued using both E Minor and E Major Blues patterns to create an unmistakable Blues/Soul vibe. Remember, blues scales are simply a pentatonic scale with an added b5 note (those added "blues notes" are indicated by hollow circles in the diagrams below).

Here are the shapes the line is built on. Note that these shapes aren't the complete patterns you'll find on the fretboard, because it's a good idea to initially restrict yourself to a few notes to get your ears and fingers around a new scale. Furthermore, players tend to build phrases around clusters or selections of notes from a scale.

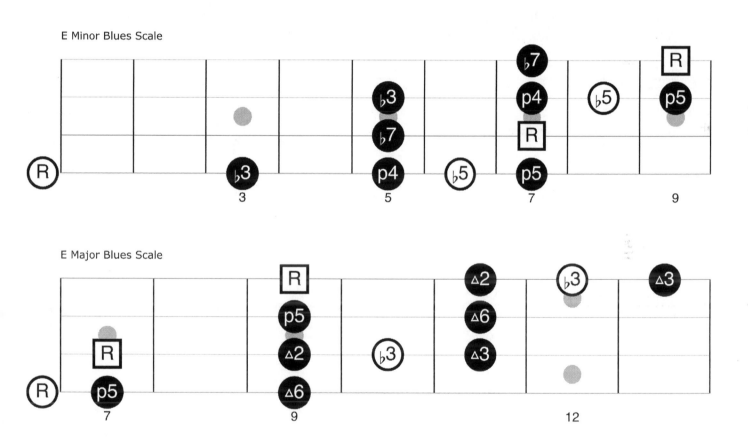

Follow the fingering pattern in bar four, shifting quickly to the 5th fret when the time comes.

The first four bars use notes from the E Minor Blues scale before switching to the major version for the next four bars. Play around with this idea of shifting major and minor harmony when you improvise.

In bar six, make sure you get the timing right with the hammer-ons, and in bar eight, slide into the 10th fret with your third finger. That's the blue note and it sounds cool!

Example 7f

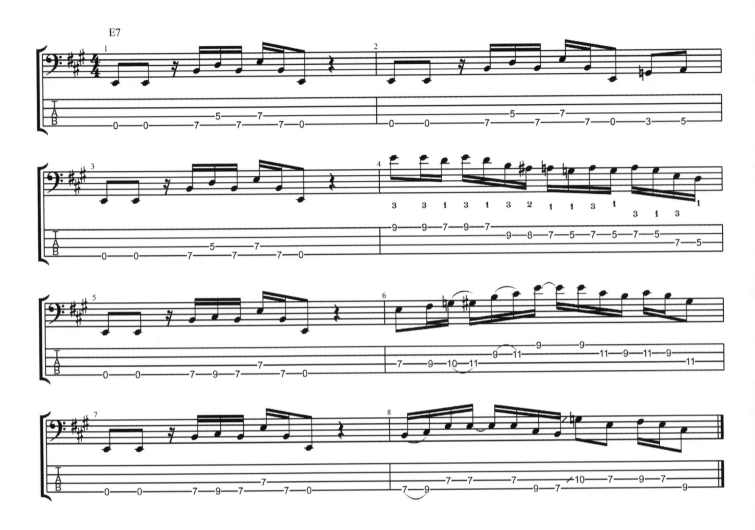

We've already encountered the pleasing sound of moving from a minor to a major third and the next example employs the same device. This time, we'll use the Dorian and the Mixolydian mode. Notice how they are *exactly* the same, apart from the 3rds. Dorian has a b3 and Mixolydian has a major 3rd.

E Dorian

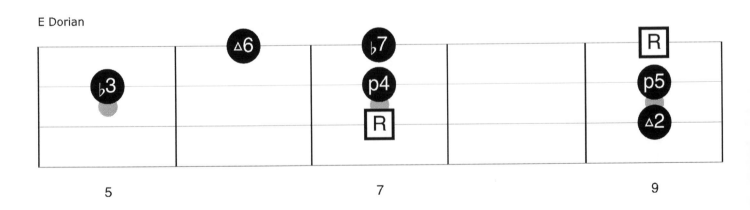

E Mixolydian

Since the rhythms are quite syncopated, I recommend studying the audio examples before attempting this example. The b7 (D) is targeted and this is a good way of moving away from the root when you stretch out in a solo.

Example 7g

The next example sticks with major harmony, using the major blues notes and highlights the major 6th (the C# on the 11th fret) and the b3 (G on the 10th fret).

In bar one, pull off from the 10th fret to the 9th with your second to first finger, before sliding immediately down to the E on the 7th fret. This should all be done in one movement and with one pluck.

Example 7h

Example 7i uses intervals to strongly outline the harmony. The notes are from the Dorian mode and the E7 arpeggio. Two notes played at the same time is called a *double-stop* and they can sound great in basslines and solos.

Root, b3, b7 from E Dorian plus a double stop (b7, Major 3rd from E7)

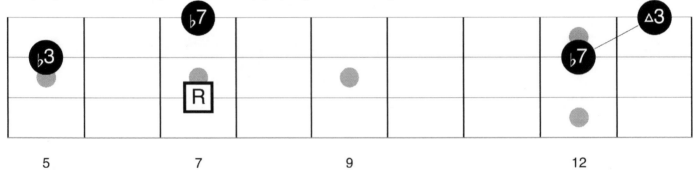

The tricky part in the next line arises in the last bar. When you play the open E, you have some time to quickly shift up for the double-stop. You need to use the same finger you used to play the D on the 7th fret for the higher note of the double-stop. I use my fourth finger, but you can use your third if you like.

Slide into the double-stop from one fret below, then slide back to the 7th fret from the 13th. You will need to do this slowly at first as it's a little awkward. If it's beyond you (for now) feel free to ignore the slide back down, shifting your hand instead. However, it's these little expressive touches that make players like Willie Weeks special and you can use them to elevate your own playing.

Example 7i

The final example uses a few of the ideas we've already seen: the b3 to major 3rd, and minor and major Blues scales. Here are the patterns presented individually.

Root, b3, Major 3rd (usually sounds best going from b3 to Major 3rd)

E Minor Blues

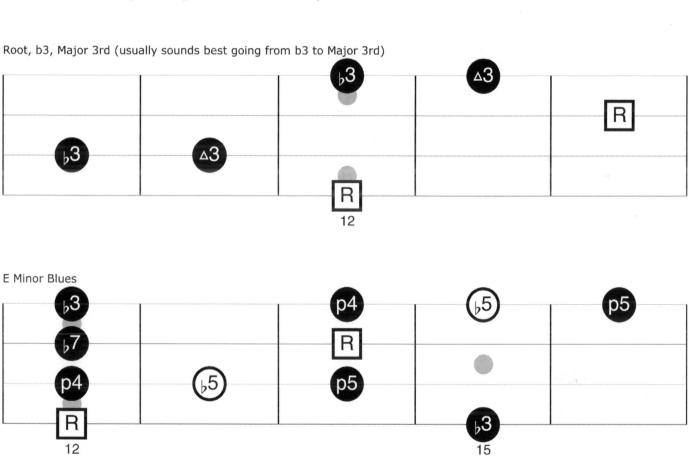

E Major Blues

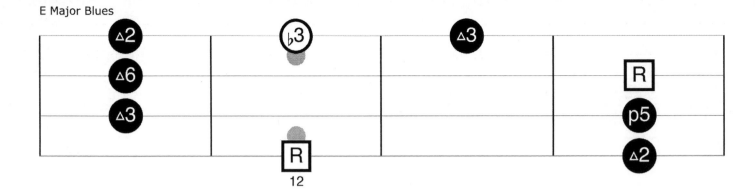

Use the rolling technique when playing the two notes on the 10th fret. Play the one on the A string with the first crease of your first finger and then roll the fingertip onto the 10th fret of the E string. Your third finger is now in position for the E on the 12th.

Example 7j

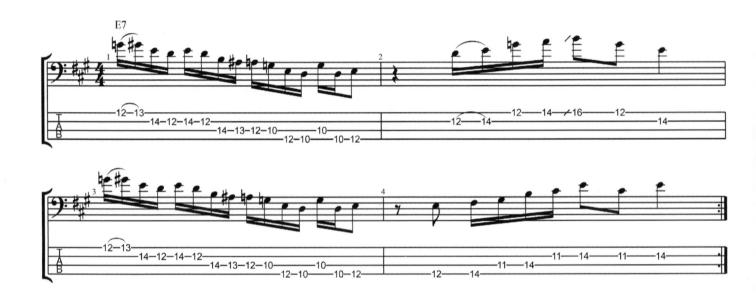

Gear Talk

You can't help but notice that most of the players in this book used a Fender Precision or a Fender Jazz. They're usually strung with flatwound strings and played through an Ampeg B15 or recorded direct through the mixing desk.

It's a simple setup but remember that the players of the 1950s didn't have much choice of gear and it's lucky that companies like Fender and Ampeg got it so right so early. You and I have more choice these days and this section takes you through some good alternative setups.

That said, please don't obsess over gear. Use whatever you have and can afford at the time. If you have a rock bass strung with stainless steel strings, you can still sound great on it. If you roll off some of the highs with the tone knob and put a foam mute by the bridge, you're ready to go. A cheap upgrade would be to string it with flatwound strings

If you are looking to go further, then read on.

Basses

Sure, you *could* just go out and buy yourself a vintage Fender Precision or Jazz and that would sound amazing. However, the pre-CBS Fenders that most players in this book originally bought fairly inexpensively are now worth tens of thousands of dollars.

The good news is that there are companies building great basses for an affordable price.

If you don't have much to spend then check out these brands:

- Sire – developed with the help of Marcus Miller and produced to high quality specs in South Korea.

- Squier – the cheaper arm of Fender. Some of the 1980s JV series ones have gone up in price but are still good value. Newer Squier models differ in quality but players including Joe Dart have used them. As with any bass, try before you buy. The Squier Classic Vibe models are quite desirable.

- Ibanez. I bought a 1982 Roadster for just over £300 and it stands up well against my '68 Precision and '75 Jazz. Japanese basses from this era can be found cheaply and help you get a vintage tone.

- Fender – there are countless newer models that you can check out.

- The Bass Centre in London make a Bass Collection Detroit bass which is cheap and excellent.

- Yamaha produce cheap basses with a variety of pickup configurations.

If money is no object, then look out for these:

- Vintage Fender Precision or Jazz. Pre CBS models cost a fortune. Some of the instruments from the late 70s and early 80s are fantastic and more affordable. Still expect to pay a few grand though.

- Olinto. Made by La Bella, these are high end vintage instruments.

- Sadowsky. Many working professionals use this excellent brand. They have a German built range that Warwick manufacture and also some more expensive New York models. Metro is their cheaper range.

The Amps

A vintage Ampeg B15 is still the holy grail of bass amps. An SVT or Fender Bassman are also era specific amps you might want to check out. All of those are available in newer models with updated technology.

In general, 15-inch speaker cabinets will get you closer to the Soul sound, as will tube amps, and there is no shortage of excellent companies to look out for, including:

- Orange

- Ashdown

- Demeter

- Audio Kitchen

- EBS

Direct Boxes

Often, Soul bassists would use the studio engineer's signal chain straight into the desk. Those old mixing desks contained analogue tube warmth that you don't get these days. However, you could opt for a DI box that allows you to plug your bass straight to the front of house desk or even your computer via an analogue to digital converter such as the Universal Audio Apollo.

Here are some great DIs to consider:

- Jules Monique. A handmade tube preamp that can connect to a power amp to run as an amp through a cabinet. Or you can just use the preamp for recording.

- ACME Motown DI. Designed to recreate the desirable colourful distortion achieved by plugging into the Motown studio's desk.

- A Designs Audio Reddi. A tube DI inspired by the Ampeg B15.

- Radial Firefly. The drive circuit on this unit features a 12AX7 tube which imparts a characterful vintage vibe.

Strings

La Bella are still considered the original and best. If you're into the old school Motown or Soul tone, then flatwounds are an important choice. Different brands do feel different, so I recommend you go into a shop and try a few out to see how they feel under your fingers.

La Bella make a heavy gauge James Jamerson set and other brands to check out include:

- Elites Detroit Flats

- Thomastik Infeld

- D'Addario Chromes

- DR Legends

Modifying Your Bass

Swapping out your original pickup can drastically improve your sound and get you closer to the vintage tone you love, and Fender make a fantastic Custom Shop '62 Fender Precision pickup. Here are some other modifications you can use to whip a cheaper bass into shape:

- Pickups. This is one of the biggest mods you can do and can have a profound effect on tone. Apart from the Fender pickup mentioned above, other great brands are Curtis Novak, Aguilar and Bareknuckle.

- Bridge. A good bridge can improve sustain, punch, and keep your bass in tune. Hipshot make excellent bridges and another classic is the Badass bridge.

- Tuners. Accurate, lightweight tuners do make a difference. Older basses especially are prone to machine heads that have worn down and are heavy and stiff.

If you're not comfortable doing any of this work yourself, take your bass to a good local luthier. They can turn your axe into a Soul sensation!

What's Next?

Now you've got the sound, techniques, style, and a bunch of basslines down, you need to immerse yourself in a deep Soul / Motown playlist so that you can absorb the attitude and vibe of this special genre of music.

Try to figure out basslines by ear and you will quickly start to recognise the shapes and patterns you've covered here. Create your own music from these patterns and use your favourite players and grooves as inspiration. The more you do this, the more you will develop your own voice. Even if you don't play Soul music, you can use many of the ideas behind these basslines in countless other styles of music.

Keep playing every day. Consistency is the key to achieving your musical goals and if I can help in any way, I'd love to hear from you. Simply get in touch via one of the channels below.

Happy bass playing!

Dan.

Connect with Dan

Instagram: **OnlineBassCourses**

YouTube: **OnlineBassCourses**

Website: **www.onlinebasscourses.com**

If you enjoyed this book, I'd be eternally grateful if you would leave an Amazon review. They massively help independent authors and allow people like me to write more books to help you on your bass playing journey.

Made in the USA
Columbia, SC
02 August 2024

39879885R00050